"Told with hard-earned confidence, [...] spirited proof that girls can dare to d[...] rivers, and wilderness—and turn those dreams into an unconventional life of adventure." —Jan Redford, author of *End of the Rope: Mountains, Marriage, and Motherhood*

"An intriguing and completely enjoyable adventure full of intimate stories. I found myself enlightened and laughing out loud at many of her predicaments. I could hardly put it down." —Brenda Stanley, author and KPVI-TV journalist

"From the straightforward introduction to the last page, this story—this honest and very personal journey—exudes strength and creativity. Kris' rich prose and insight reel you in—not unlike her photos themselves—and then let you think about your own possibilities." —Rebecca Casper, Idaho Falls Mayor

"This book is the backstory—the outtakes—of the most incredible news stories Millgate has reported on. From tackling deer to filming wildfire, the plots turn personal, as she lets us in on the secrets of how she overcame her childhood shyness and fear of beards to become an award-winning journalist." —Emily M. Stone, author of *Natural Connections: Exploring Northwoods Nature through Science and Your Senses*

"Kris puts you into each scene with an easy, expressive style—and she's not afraid to deliver a truth along the way. She provides a blueprint for the next generation of brave, caring young women to make a difference in the outdoors." —Bruce Reichert, Idaho Public Television executive producer and Outdoor Idaho host

"This remarkable book is a testament to human perseverance, both personal and professional. It's also a testament to the healing powers of America's wild places. Above all, it's a call to live life on your terms and to savor every bit of it."
—Slaton L. White, *Field & Stream* contributing editor

"In her new book, Kris Millgate proves that being a freelancing outdoor journalist, especially a female one in a male-dominated field, is no vacation. Fueled by passion and grit, Millgate shares how she's courageously pushed through her childhood shyness and on-the-job challenges—including birds, bears, a broken leg, bad dreams, and beards—in hot pursuit of stories that inspire others to understand, enjoy, and treasure the Great Outdoors."
—Colleen Miniuk, outdoor photographer, writer, and founder of Sheography™

"*My Place Among Men* is about Kris Millgate never giving in and keeping faith in herself across decades of hard work and artistic pursuit. She defined success for herself and hunted it down with relentless ardor. There's a trove of lessons in that no matter your gender or work environment."
—T. Edward Nickens, *Field & Stream* editor-at-large

"Millgate transcended this male-dominated niche in a way that I can only hope will resonate for generations, and inspire other young women to follow. The work speaks for itself. Amazing."
—Kirk Deeter, *Trout Media* editor-in-chief

"I am so happy that Kris put down in words what most women have never experienced working in a man's world of outdoor video production." —Sauni Symonds, Idaho Public TV-Outdoor Idaho lead producer

MY PLACE AMONG MEN

MISADVENTURES IN THE WILD

BY KRIS MILLGATE

Published by Inkshares, Inc., Oakland, California
www.inkshares.com

Cover design by Tim Barber of Dissect Designs
Interior design by Kevin G. Summers

ISBN: 9781950301010
e-ISBN: 9781950301027
LCCN: 2019932427

First edition

Printed in the United States of America

Dedicated to my three "home" boys. One with a beard. Two without. They live with me, laugh with me, and love me. Even when I expect adventures that are beyond reasonable.

PROLOGUE

Grow Girl

AS A LITTLE GIRL, I was shy. Painfully shy. Eye contact? Out of the question. Talking? No way. Strangers never heard my voice, especially strangers with hair on their faces.

Beards terrified me. It's a quirk from birth like being a lefty, which I am. Beards have no traumatic moment of specific blame for my aversion, but unlike my dominant left hand, my anti-beard stance changed when I stepped outside.

Now I talk so much, I have swollen vocal cords and I run around in the wild daily with beards. It just goes to show what a determined young girl will overcome when she knows without any doubt that she's going to tell you a story when she grows up. More on that later, but let's grow this girl first.

I didn't grow up fishing or hunting with my dad; I hiked with my dad. Endlessly. My mom says I don't have a danger gene. Well, my dad doesn't have an internal compass. He's always lost and never admitting it. Our hikes in Utah's Wasatch Mountains were endless wanders—peppercorn-speckled granite crawling up one canyon, red-brown blend spilling down the other. That's the allure of Little and Big Cottonwood Canyons east of Salt Lake City.

In those steep canyons, I spent a pile of miserable miles staring at the back of my dad, his head shaded by a ball cap, his pocketknife sheathed on his belt. He'd declare "Just around the next bend" every five minutes, and I'd spend the next four minutes doubting him. The combination of his declaration and my doubt taught me patience in an unexpected way. Despite my doubt, I kept hiking with him, and misery turned majestic.

With my dad, I learned to pack along endurance and persistence, too. Quitters on those two fronts won't see the country my dad wanders: acres of aspen cleared by an avalanche, five bull moose bedded around one snow-fed lake, and the ever-gaping hole he told me was an ancient volcano but is really just a hot spring.

I still practice patience for the wild's antics. Animals don't conveniently do something cool in front of my lens just because I want them to. Half the time they don't even step into view let alone do something worth watching.

As for the other two traits I learned while trailing my dad, my endurance will exhaust you and my persistence will intimidate you. Both have to if I'm going to make it among those who claim my chosen line of work is no place for a lady.

The boys tried locking their clubhouse door but I kicked it in, and what I discovered is an outdoor playground worthy of report. That playground includes watching men cry in the middle of rivers, throw fits when they miss a shot, and pummel Road Closed signs. I join their laughter for no reason and for good reason. And I give them space when gender differences prove too much for them.

I'm a rarity in the woods and in my profession. Women are underrepresented in the outdoors, especially in outdoor journalism. But I'm not here because I'm rare. I'm here because the best stories are in the wild and those are the stories I tell—tears, fists, and fits included.

I'm honored when men invite me to sit around their campfires, fish from their boats, and explore their favorite trails. Together we marvel at mass migrations, raging rivers, and scorching wildfires. We admire rising suns, swirling snowflakes, and open country. We also share in our struggles with personal baggage, inner demons, and unfulfilled ambitions.

As an outdoor journalist, it's my job—shy tendencies aside—to find the story and tell it. Vividly. Accurately. Drop me in unknown places full of unknown faces and I'll find you a story. My gender is irrelevant when it comes to my skills; all you need to know is that I carry my own weight and I do my job well.

The result of my relentless pursuit to work where most women won't is this: I know more about fishin' than fashion, I'll show you my boots but never my boobs, and I don't want to hold your hand, so don't try to hold mine.

Oh, one more thing. I'm not after a date—I'm after a story.

Turns out, the story is mine.

CONTENTS

PART I

Hiding

DREAMING BIG

CLAWS AND JAWS.

I'm concerned about both. I only see one: claws. Not friendly, kitty-cat claws. These are fear-inducing grizzly bear claws and I'm holding them. I'm not bumfuzzled or bold. I'm an outdoor journalist with the dream job. Well, my dream job. Most other women don't consider the squalor of the stinky wild dreamy, but I do.

Bears do stink and they do hog the top spot on my bucket list. Especially when I'm on assignment and the bear is out cold. The sleepy-time shot to its shoulder has it under a spell that makes it possible for me to safely shoot close-up footage while researchers examine this four-year-old bear.

A bear's teeth are tucked in when it sleeps, but its claws are always out. That's probably why I take so many pictures of claws. They don't retract like a cat's. It's like trying to pal around with Wolverine when he's mad—blades out and ready.

The visual intensity makes my hands rattle, but I work through it. At least I think I do. Most of my shots for this story are steady while I lie on my belly nose to nose with Grizzly No. 1,225. His breathing is slow and deep. Mine is quick and shallow. My hyped rhythm races to hysteria when the bear's eyelids flip open.

"He's up!" I say with blurted surprise, while also peeing my pants. A lot. It's true, but at least that's all I did.

Eye twitch is normal, I'm told. The ticker tells us we still have ten minutes of sedation. It's just enough time to bolt on the GPS collar, so I keep working on footage.

I'm filling frame with the beautiful beast's signature shoulder hump when the bear lifts its head. I lift mine in alarm.

"No!" I say. "He's really up!"

I rise to run. The bear rises to chase. The fall comes twelve paces after the chase starts.

I wake up freaked out, fur still filling my head. But the fear is fading. Falling dreams are the worst, the quick tensing of every muscle in your body painfully jerking you from sleeping to waking in an agonizing instant. You acknowledge the ache right away. Recognizing the dream is secondary.

That's right, I was dreaming. No bear, no chase, no fall. I didn't even get up for a potential fall, but I have to get up now.

"I'm fine," I say, rising from the couch, straddling my body with crutches and moving through the kitchen. "I'm not having a come-apart."

My head hits the door.

I'm not fine. I'm having a come-apart.

My head hits the door again.

"I thought you just said you were fine," my husband says from the kitchen table, with his morning mug of liquid magic that I love to smell but hate to taste.

"But the door is closed," I say with a sob. Not a whine, a sob.

My husband leaves his coffee cup and reaches me in two strides. My head is still leaning on the door. My eyes are down, tears dripping onto my swollen purple toes.

"I'll get the door for you," he says with a chuckle. He quickly follows this with "I'm not laughing at you. I'm laughing with you."

"But I'm not laughing," I say, switching from sob to sober. "I'm about to shit myself and the door is closed."

My leg is broken in three places. I'm heavily sedated and couch bound. I haven't done serious bathroom business for more than a week. This is a significant moment in my recovery and I'm stopped at a closed door. It's a swinging door, separating kitchen from laundry room and half bath.

Swinging doors don't have knobs. They don't need them. Just give a nudge with your hand or hip and what's closed easily swings open in either direction. Perfect for when your hands are full—full of anything but crutches.

My bruised palms are gripping crutches. There's no nudging the door open with hand or hip. Between the crutches are my grossly mismatched lower limbs. The left leg is beefed up like a brute dead-lifting all 125 pounds of me. The right leg, the one that's all wrong, is shriveled and useless. It's broken, so there's no kicking the door open either.

The reality of a disability, even a temporary one, is humbling in so many ways that it becomes unnerving. Friends check in on me and say, "I miss you." I miss me too. I'm reduced from living life amplified to stopped at a single door, exhausted by the thought of getting through it.

The only thing I can push the door open with is my head and that takes forever. I'll never make it. I'll poop in the shorts I've worn for a week and my husband will have yet another thing to do for me since I can't do a single thing for myself.

Smiling, he swings the door wide, silently props it open, and then politely steps aside so my crippled gait has plenty of hobbling space. I pass him, the washing machine, and the dryer. Next, coats, boots, and baskets full of beanies and gloves. One more hop and I'm in the half bath. It has a sliding door. I force my sore left armpit to suction cup the top of my left crutch. I release my left hand from its bruising hold on the middle handle of the same crutch. I slowly slide the door closed with my stiff fingers, lean both crutches on the counter, and then lower myself one-legged onto the toilet.

I made it. I'm shaking and sweating, but I made it. And I'm nearly lucid, so I'm not dizzy as my left leg settles into seated position while my right leg extends straight out, bloody and bruised with every color but healthy. It hovers two inches above the bathroom rug. My husband hovers two feet outside the door.

Even in my hallucinogenic state, I think he's handsome, maybe more so. Drugs do that. He's handsome, not handy. I've always said hire handy, marry handsome. And that's exactly what I did.

Women raised my husband, so he doesn't leave the toilet seat up. He knows how to cook and he has great fashion sense.

When we were younger, his dark hair was so groomed, it was glossy. He wore it longer then. Now it's short and textured with the color of age, but no less appealing. It still complements his sharp cheekbones and his lips, perfected with a slight pout. The whole façade is confidently roughed with a short-trimmed, almost stubble-length beard. I love that beard. Crazy to think I once feared beards and now I'm married to a marvelous one.

"See, no poopy pants, babe. You made it," he says from the other side of the door. "And I'm still right here when you need me."

With him it's never *if you need me*. It's when. When. Not if. Always when, and for this *when*, I'm taking him for all he's worth.

SKATING AWAY

MY HUSBAND COACHES youth hockey and so do I, but that's not what we do for a living. He's a behaviorist who works with special needs students in the public school system. I'm a journalist who works with wild things in wild places. When we're not wrapped up in what dominates our professional lives, our two boys who play hockey dictate our personal time.

A week ago my husband and I were both on the ice, but he was standing on it and I was lying on it. Neither of us grew up playing hockey, but we'd rather be on the bench than in the stands, so we learned to skate then learned the game. I coach our youngest. My husband coaches our eldest. We aren't head coach material—we leave that to the guys who grew up on the ice. They know hockey. We know kids. It works now. But the first year, it didn't.

In our first year of coaching, my husband walked into the coaches' locker room, found unoccupied space on the bench, and sat down to change from shoes to skates. When I first walked into the coaches' locker room, I found an angry hockey player in not-so-tighty whities yelling about how he wasn't having any of this. I was the "this."

He was trying to humiliate me. It worked. He was the one standing in public in his underwear, yet I was the one humiliated. I didn't want to be, but I couldn't rein in my initial reaction. Humiliated—shocked, too—but mostly humiliated. Stripping down to nearly naked on the pretense of a normal occurrence in the men's locker room was his way of telling me he didn't consider the coaches' locker room coed. His skin statement meant he didn't want me around. Frankly, I didn't want to be around. Who would, for that? I hated how he raised the response he'd expected, humiliation, but I made sure I didn't give him the result he'd expected: surrender.

He was as defensive as anyone in briefs could be. I was as offended as any other woman in our coed locker room should be. Wait. There weren't any other women. It was coed by regulation, but not by ritual. I left the locker room, laced up my skates in the lobby, and started coaching. Undies on the Defense laced up his shoes, left the rink, and stopped coaching.

Fast-forward a few years and I'm still the only woman in the coed locker room for the age group I coach, but more moms are following suit in younger divisions. I purposely sit by the locker room door so anyone coming in knows right away this particular hockey program is coed in writing and in reality. Panty parties, defensive or otherwise, are not allowed, and the rapport between coaches is respectful, if not also hilarious. We're a funny lot unless one of us goes down. This time it's me that goes down. I took a puck to the shin last week. The impact did more damage than anyone anticipated.

Five minutes into practice and halfway through our six-month-long season, my right leg crumbles when I hockey-stop. I mean, it just crumbles. Like back-of-the-cupboard stale, crusty, bottom-of-the-bag cookies that taste as bad as they look so they're better off in the garbage than in your mouth.

Or maybe the other kind of crumble. The spectacular Vegas-building-blowup kind: picture the implosion of a hotel casino as it collapses. That's what the bones between my knee and ankle do. Implosions spread, too, dust and debris billowing out the bottom of the crumble pile. My leg does just that, sending pain beyond tolerable reason tingling down to my toes and up past my knee.

I lie there post-implosion. The men, including my husband, stand there. Dust dropping, tingles fizzling, crumble settling. Me looking up, them looking down. The scenario is similar to the first story I wrote in journalism school at the University of Utah, titled "Glass Floor."

The story was about the limits of career-oriented women being capped by a glass floor instead of a glass ceiling. My argument stated that a floor, not a ceiling, separates genders in the professional realm. Women are under a floor of glass gawking up at a million pairs of finely polished Sunday shoes. The shoes belong to businessmen climbing the corporate ladder while barefoot, pregnant women who want careers, but have kids instead, stare from the basement through the glass floor overhead.

I wanted to punch that glass, steal those shoes, and climb that ladder with a camera in my hand and a kid on my back. Both. It's both. It's not one or the other. No *or*. It's *and*. And it is possible. Watch me rise. When, not if.

I'm deep in that crusade when a bout of vomit immediately brings me back to the present, the present state of a pathetic girl sprawling awkwardly on the ice. The men stare down at me, confused. There's no cap on me here, there's no division between us, no gender struggle. There's no businessman halting my progress, holding me back, stopping my go by stepping on me with recently shined Sunday shoes. There are only skates, ice, and faces as I look up in agony.

The pain of such a sorry state is so overwhelming, sour juices of adrenaline rise from my gut. I'm still wearing a helmet and my helmet includes a mask of crossbars designed to protect my moneymaking TV face from pucks. Puking inside a face mask has no benefits, so I swallow excess spit and squeeze my eyes shut.

No one pushed me down. I fell, that's all. I fell and mercy, this fall hurts. The queen mother of all cuss words breathlessly slips like cold mist out of my mouth, and they're still staring, you know, like men do when the hood is up on a car that has a smoking engine?

Their helmeted faces, some bearded and some not, huddle above me, silently assessing for a split second then realizing no one knows why I won't get up, so everyone starts spouting questions. Questions for which I have no answers, because anguish is stealing my awareness. Then little faces push into the huddle and I find my voice. I find it fast.

"Get the kids off the ice," I say, through gritted teeth. "All of them. Off. Now."

I'm the coach who doesn't yell and doesn't cuss. I need to yell loudly and I need to cuss hard, but I must delay both until all the kids are off the ice. The tether keeping my back flat on the blue line and my mouth closed within the cage of my helmet is dangerously thin, shredded from strain. It's going to snap and I'm going to lose it.

The kids get off as more men enter the huddle. Hockey dads shouldering in with hockey coaches to look at what's lying limp at the wrong angle under the proverbial hood. No one knows how to fix me.

Ambulance it is, but I can't tell you a single thing about the ride. I don't remember it. I wasn't mentally there, but my husband was. Between panicked punching and bouts of breath holding, I yelled and cussed all the way to the emergency room. He told me I did and he knows because he stayed.

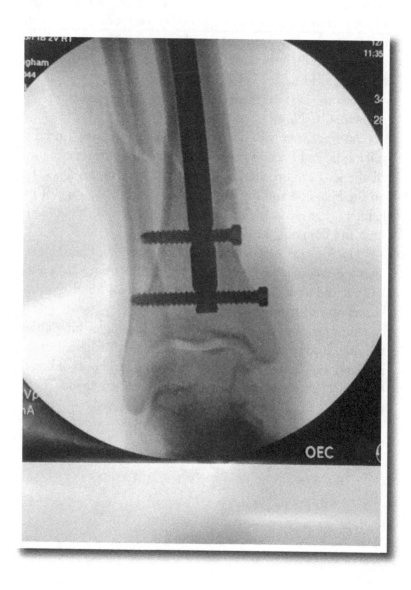

STAYING DESPITE LEAVING

THE NEXT THING I remember is a heavy skate. It's flopping around on a table, blade stabbing close to all the hands helping in the ER. They're trying to get the skate off my fat foot attached to my disconnected leg and it's not going well.

Hey! Did you say "disconnected?" I'm beyond worrying about kids hearing me cuss now. How in the hell am I going to chase wildlife with a disconnected leg? Shattered parts don't make it outside. They die outside or stay inside. I'll die inside if I can't be outside. Disconnected, busted, broken, useless. None of it is for me, but I'm pretty sure it's my leg they're yanking because I don't feel good at all.

My husband doesn't feel good either. I can tell because he's looking at my face instead of my feet. He's telling me to breathe. "What? Breathe? I'm not having a baby! I'm holding my breath because this ordeal hurts way more than having a baby. Now put my leg back on and let's get the hell out of here," I tell him.

My demands—or maybe the scene—is so unbearable, my husband steps away from the operating table, takes off a few layers of clothing, holds his head for a few seconds, then steps back in with tell-it-like-it-is resolve.

He says it's worse than when I tore a ligament in my left knee during a mountain bike wreck with my yellow Lab, Caddis. It's worse than when I threw up on him in bed multiple times. And worse, way worse, than watching me have both of our boys. I agree on all accounts.

I mean, parts go weird ways when birthing babies, but they go right back after pushing. All the pushing in the world isn't putting any of my leg back. A needle pokes my lower spine. Morphine lubes my veins. Panic and pain fade to black.

A few hours later, I startle myself out of a falling dream with a holler. My husband lets me know he's in the room and the surgery is done. He can't look at my leg anymore, so he's in a chair on my left side, nearly behind my bed. Even when he doesn't speak, I know he's there by the sound of his body shifting in the uncomfortable seat. Hospital chairs aren't meant for staying, but my husband stays. My dad doesn't.

He arrives with three orange roses in a red vase, kisses my forehead, and says there's nowhere else he'd rather be than with me. Pretty sure that's what he says, but that's not what he means.

In all fairness, medicine makes me lose my mind and I have an unreliable memory during extreme pain. I don't pass out, but I don't remember most of the moments within it either. The moment must be emotionally rough to be remembered, and just ten minutes after my dad arrives, it's emotionally rough indeed. I know it is, because I remember it.

He looks at the clock.

"Nearly noon," he says, still wearing his coat. "I have to leave."

His wife needs a ride home from work. In Utah. We're in Idaho. He drove three hours with three roses to stay for ten minutes? He's leaving? Already?

He does win points for showing up. Let's say ten, one point for each minute. He's ten points ahead of everyone else in my family. My sister asked how she could help from here, with here being Utah. My mother is MIA and my brother mailed me a bell, like a dinner bell or service bell. I am to ring it when I need something. Pretty funny actually, but for some reason when I ring, he doesn't appear. That part isn't funny, actually. He must not be able to hear the bell across the border of our neighboring states. All right, I get it. Everyone has more important people to tend to and I'm not dying. I just feel like I am. Excessive pain makes me a bit dramatic, but in all seriousness I am sad that the family who made me isn't here for me.

Trouble is, my husband thinks my dad is here to help. I think my dad is here because I matter most, but we're both wrong. The realization is beyond awful. It's emotionally rough. My dad leaves the hospital. My husband leaves the room. Time and tears pass. My husband returns with a wheelchair and kindly says, "Let's go." My dad is off his radar as fast as medicine erases my memory.

"I'll skip work and stay with you," he says, gathering a pile of papers and prescriptions. "Through puke, through pain, we'll get through this. You'll be back to being you with both legs working, and I'll be there when that happens."

When, not if. Just like that, he always reassures me. *When*, not if. I don't know when, but there is no if.

I'm working on *when* as I crutch my way back from the bathroom through the now stuck-open swinging door. I pass my smiling husband with his coffee in the kitchen and drop myself onto the couch.

The couch is where I spend my days while my husband misses work without missing a single dose of the medicine he's in charge of giving me. The thick-cushioned black couch was a beloved wedding gift from his sister and brother-in-law two decades ago. It has moved across the country and back. It has held babies and boys and now it holds me, with my thin, twiggy limb elevated and unprotected. No boot, no cast.

My tibia is broken in one place, my fibula in two. Doc opened my knee to hammer . . . yes, hammer. Pause, breathe, get a grip on the grossness of that. Hammer a titanium rod into my tibia. That's the big bone, the front of your shin. The two breaks in my fibula—the smaller bone to the side of, and a bit behind, the tibia—are free-floating. Those breaks need stillness to mend. Binding my leg to hold one break puts too much pressure on another break, so exposed it is with random strands of bloody surgery gauze clinging to places I'm not allowed to soak in the tub.

I recently shot footage of a one-legged sparrow eating seed on a sidewalk. The strength of its one leg admirable, its still-alive status unbelievable. Two-legged birds have plenty of predators. Double that for a one-legged bird, but this one avoids being prey. So do I . . . or at least I will as soon as my Humpty Dumpty deformity is back together again and I can go outside.

Looking at footage of the one-legged sparrow now makes me uncomfortable. The absence of a lower part turning from fascinating to freaky as I realize I shot the footage just two months before I'm reduced to one leg, feathers foreshadowing my fate.

There's a titanium rod inside my leg. My body wants to spit it out. I picture frost spreading along the rod as my husband refills ice packs and returns them to my shin, my calf, my knee, and my ankle.

There are three screws in my leg too. Two above my ankle and one below my knee. They hold the rod in place. My body doesn't want those, either. I picture them unwinding as my mind unravels with another dose of Percocet for pain, Phenergan for puke, diazepam for spasms, aspirin for clots, ibuprofen for whatever I want, and stool softener for . . . well, I already told you about that mandatory doctor-documented moment officially starting my recovery. Sometimes I can leave the couch, but most of the time I stay and so does my husband.

FOLLOWING FIT

FROM THE COUCH I see several artistic canvas wraps on the walls of my home. They're images I've shot while on assignment and blown up larger than life for others to inspect. Some are for sale, and some are for myself.

"Power House" is one of my favorites and it's one of my oldest pieces. It's a photo I shot of a bald eagle on a power pole in 2010. I had it transferred to a poster-sized canvas and it hangs near the main entryway into our home.

"Power House" started the collection I call "Bring Outside In." The collection, including pieces that hang in other people's homes and offices, is my way of helping you experience the outdoors when you aren't outside or, in some cases, when you don't feel comfortable outside. Look at a picture of wild long enough and, if it's shot right, you're going to want to *be* in that place, not just looking at it.

My hope is that by sharing wildlife and wild lands as art, rather than just news, more people will want to experience the natural world for themselves or at least find it interesting enough to pay attention to it when it's in the news. People don't protect what they don't know, so I want all genders and all ages to know our natural world, to know what wet bark smells like and to know what dry earth feels like. Showing people what outside looks like when they're inside is a start. If you want to know what the unfolding wings of the bald eagle in "Power House" sound like, step outside.

"Power House" reminds me of being nine. It's early spring and I'm running in from recess smelling of slippery mud and saturated grass. I pitch my rain jacket on a hallway hook in Philo T. Farnsworth Elementary and line up. (The irony of growing up in a school named after the father of television is not lost on me.)

I'm painfully shy and fiercely quiet, so I easily settle down and fall in line just as our fourth-grade teacher, Mr. Mietchen, asks. He is feather-haired and has a mustache (but no beard).

My obedience puts me at the head of the order, which also puts me in the front row once we reach the gym. We sit criss-cross applesauce on a tiled floor that reeks of ketchup and tots. The gym is also the lunchroom. It works, but it's not the best fit—kind of like me. I don't really fit. The unsettled burden of unfit eases if I lower my eyes, so that's what I do. Often.

I have a formidable relationship with my shoes. I always look down at them so I don't have to make eye contact with you. I figure if I can't see you, you can't see me. Seems silly, but it works in my head. My belt-length light-brown hair follows lowered eyes, filling peripheral leaks left and right. Braided or brushed out, its length reinforces my "hiding" from others. And I do hide. It's just how I'm wired.

I sit as assigned, picking blades of grass out of my sneaker bottoms. Octagonal chunks of recently thawed earth lift from the soles. The beige blend of ground matches the pant legs of the man walking into the gym. I hear gasps around me and decide the audibles warrant my attention more than my shoes do.

I raise my hesitant hazel eyes to study what's in the spotlight. It's an ordinary, no-beard man wearing a wide-brimmed hat on his head and a tree patch on his sleeve. The ordinary man is holding something extraordinary: a bald eagle. Sugar-white head, chocolate-brown body, banana-yellow eyes. I have no idea who the man is, but he's beardless, so he must tell truths. Beards don't tell truths; clean faces always do.

I go to church with clean faces. My dad has a clean face. Clean faces are honest. I've known this as long as I've known that Saturday is a special day, because it's the day we get ready for Sunday. As the Mormon church hymn goes, we brush our clothes and shine our shoes so we can be ready for Sunday. The shaving part of that song isn't mentioned because it's done on Sunday, not Saturday. It has to be done on Sunday morning so you don't have stubble showing during church services.

The most faithful members are clean-shaven on Sunday and every other day. My dad is faithful. My teacher probably is too. They're both beardless truth-tellers. The man with the bird on his arm is beardless too, so he must have a truth to tell.

"Take a good look at this bird," he says, raising the bird, its talons wrapped tightly around his arm. "It's the last time you will see it. Bald eagles will disappear by the time you grow up."

My timid eyes take in the bird's bold eyes and I inwardly squirm, thinking to myself, "If something this awesome isn't going to make it here, how on earth am I going to make it?"

I don't know anything about the endangered species list for disappearing animals, but I do know that this bird is on it and has been since the year I was born. The ordinary man holding the extraordinary bird says so.

I don't know anything about the pesticide problem that put bald eagles on that list either, but I know I'm looking at something no one should erase and everyone should see. Me, the shy girl sitting crisscross in the front row, says so.

I'm still thinking about that bird, its eyes up toward the horizon, on my walk home from school. It's a decent walk from the bus stop, but I know the safety of this suburb well, so awareness slips as I hop cracks in the sidewalk.

I live in a typical neighborhood trimmed with fences, flowers, and stay-at-home moms. Except for my mom, who works. I'm a latchkey kid, wearing the key to my house around my neck on a shin's length of hot-pink yarn.

The yarn is tucked inside my rain jacket sprinkled with March moisture. My hood is up and my eyes are down, as usual. I'm in my head, but I'm not walking alone. At least not by the appearance of things. Two girls, besties, are a step ahead of me. I'm the third wheel, always. I want so badly to fit in that I shadow people who seem to fit in. I settle for the back seat, hoping the girls will fight, like girls do, and then I'll hop in the front seat, shoulder to shoulder where best friends walk instead of behind.

The besties turn the block and I go straight. My driveway is four houses down. Wouldn't it be cool if a bald eagle were perched on my porch? It's not, but there's a cardboard box by the front door. I hate that box. It's food, donated food, left by the lady at church who is in charge of those who need charity but don't ask for it. Why is it there if we don't ask? I only ask myself that, because I don't yet have the voice to question the unwelcome delivery out loud. Truth be told, my mom, in a desperate measure due to a marriage on the rocks, probably did ask for help and I just don't know it. All I know is I certainly didn't ask for help.

Now don't misunderstand me here: I love food, but not the food in that cardboard box. That food lingers on our front porch, an emblem of my family's shortcomings for the entire neighborhood to see. Needing help, relying on others—our inability to make it without help—embarrasses me. It mortifies me to have that damn box of charity left on my porch.

I'm not supposed to swear, but my mom says *damn* so I say it, too. She says it with the kind of flare I hope to inherit one day, so I put in a lot of damn practice. Damn that box and damn the food inside it, especially the milk. That damn donation milk with the lame light-blue cow on the carton makes me mad and fearful. I fear that someday, when I'm fit enough to have friends over, one of them will want cookies and milk while we're hanging out and they'll see that damn cow on the carton, exposing my weakness. It's my family's plight, really, but it feels like mine alone.

The limbo status of my parents' on-and-off love affair means my dad's dollars aren't always in our house. My parents both work and sometimes their marriage works, but when it doesn't, I feel even more unfit.

Mormon families don't split. They're meant to be together forever according to another church song I learned at age five that makes me cry when we sing it on Sundays. Only forever families go to heaven.

Divorced families don't go to heaven, so why is the *D*-word debated in my house? Why are my parents even considering it? There's no divorce. Just like there are no beards. Worthy male members don't divorce, don't have beards, and they're blessed with special privileges, like Scout camp. I hate Scout camp. My dad and brother get to go, but I don't get to go. Girls aren't allowed at Scout camp. I don't want to sell cookies—I want to catch fish, but I can't go.

I hate the word *can't*, too. And *quit*. I don't use either unless I'm using them together: *can't quit*. I tell myself that a lot. I can't quit. Quitters don't fit and one day I'm going to fit, just as sure as that damn cow on the carton of milk won't be on my doorstep when I grow up. And I'll say *damn* with flare.

I avoid eye contact with the cardboard box and the cow it contains, circle the house, and open the back door with my house key hanging on yarn. My mom can bring in the charity. I might not fit yet, but the food in that box isn't mine.

SIBLINGS AND SUCH

A FEW DAYS later those two girls, the besties walking one step ahead me, fight. I don't understand why they fight over Barbies and boys. I don't really care why, as long as they fight. When they fight, I'm their new best friend. I vacate third-wheel status and move up shoulder to shoulder. I go to their houses to play instead of having them over to mine. I don't want them to see that damn cow on the carton of milk.

I enjoy bestie status every few weeks. That's progress. I'm figuring out this "fit" thing. I have friends, either one of the girls when the besties fight. And boys—boys who don't fight over Barbies, boys who my little brother befriends. Derk, Berny, Booger. Booger is Mikey. That's my angel-eyed baby brother. We're close in age, but not in priority. He's the only son my dad always wanted, but my sister was born first.

Angie's five years ahead of me, with boyfriends, girl friends, and a closet full of clothes I wish I fit in. She's the "one" child my mom wanted.

And then there's me, the middle child. Not the only son or the only child. I know I'm loved by my family and that jokes about me being the deprived middle child are just jokes, but deep down, the mark of middle feeds my motivation to force my way into a place where I fit.

My pursuit of that place suffers a setback the day my parents stop debating the *D*-word and officially divorce. My dad runs off with a new wife and doesn't come back. And he grows a beard. My mom runs to her room and doesn't come out. She cries, too. Her solitary sorrow spreads through our home's heat vents like my dad's classical music used to rise from his basement den, where he drafted dreams on paper.

My dad is a friendly man who means well. His intentions are sometimes misguided, but always sincere in delivery. He loves religion and spends more time thinking about the afterlife than living this life. My mom is just the opposite: she spends more time lamenting the past than creating a future.

I'm disappointed and sad when I look at my parents, exposed by the harsh glare of reality, not because of who they are, but because of what they struggle with. They struggle with

their definition of success and their inability to achieve it. My dad's success, eternal life, is only possible beyond death, and my mom's closest brush with success, the storybook family, didn't last. They don't know I see their anxiety over their shortcomings, but I do. I see it manifest in every life choice, big or small, in every argument, every sigh, and even in the pauses between their sentences.

My shy avoidance of others is a protection measure, but it's also a diversion. I study people. They think that when I lower my eyes I'm done looking, but I'm not. When people look away, I study everything about them: voice delivery, facial expressions, hand gestures, obvious insecurities, hidden meanings. I study it all, choose the strongest traits for fitting in, then add those to my mental list of who to mimic, how to be, and what to hide.

I think about hiding inside my curtain of hair in high school, but I don't let myself do it. I fit. Not just some of the time, but most of the time. I try out for the dance team and the cheer squad. I make dance a year ahead of cheer, but stick with cheer when I win that fit.

By my senior year, I'm head cheerleader and homecoming queen, but I don't have a date. My friends are boy friends. Boy friends don't take girl friends to the homecoming dance. They take *girlfriends*. Fortunately, football player Danny doesn't have a girlfriend, so he takes me, his girl friend. We fit the part, but we don't kiss.

The guy I really want to kiss doesn't show up at school very often. He's in my math class sporadically and in the halls occasionally. He cares less about fitting in than anyone I've ever studied. Probably because he fits in a way that can't be matched. He's unfiltered and beardless with nothing to hide. His parents are divorced, but it doesn't matter. He doesn't go to church, but who cares? Where will he be this weekend? Where everyone else wants to be. His lack of needing to fit makes him fit in a way I envy. He's not my first kiss, but he's my first-date kiss.

My first kiss happened around the same time I was learning about eagles in elementary school. It was BJ. Our sisters were the same age and had the same name, so when the Angies hung out, BJ and I hung out.

One summer afternoon, he was peeling an orange at his kitchen sink. We were taking a break from jumping on the trampoline outside. I was standing rinse-side, and his arms were in the wash-side. We were shoulder to shoulder, best buddies joking about first kisses. We decided to be each other's firsts. No tongue, mostly cheek. It was clumsy, but tender. It was significant in its simplicity. To this day, it's what I think about every time I smell citrus.

The first time someone kisses me on a first date is a whole different deal, a bigger-than-big deal. It's a few months after the homecoming dance with that boy friend of mine who I didn't kiss. And it's after the guy says good night. After. Not like in the movies when it is the good night. It's after the good night, no more discussion, and I'm almost through the door.

We lost our house when my parents divorced, so it's the first time a boy picks me up for a date at an apartment complex. I'm embarrassed by our housing status like I'm embarrassed by light-blue cows on cartons of charity milk. The lady who delivers that milk lost track of us in the move, so there's no cardboard box of food on our porch anymore. In fact, there is no front porch at all. Just a mash of buildings with stacks of stairs leading to every door but the one that leads to heaven. That door isn't here. Divorced families are here, but he who is also of a *D*-word family doesn't care.

He drops me off after our first date, an evening of watching John Hughes movies and also watching his best friend make out with some girl. He follows me up the stairs, says good night, turns away, and then turns back. I'm fumbling, head down, with the key I don't carry on yarn anymore, when he lifts my chin and leans in. No tongue, all lip. A better goodbye after the verbal one. He smells of wood and tastes like mint. I see the sparkle of his metal retainer on his lower teeth as we finish our first-date kiss.

I know there will be a next-date kiss, and he knows it, too. His eyes-up no-shy confidence makes me stagger in senior hall. His I-don't-care-what-you-think confidence makes my pom-poms and crown seem like ridiculous rewards for what I thought was fit.

FRAMING A FUTURE

YOU KNOW THE "most likely" labels in yearbooks? Those "most likely to succeed" sort of honors? I have one, but it doesn't feel like an honor. It feels like a cross to bear and I don't want to bear it.

The week of high school graduation, I hear I'm most likely to marry right after high school and have babies before I'm of legal drinking age. I'm devastated by the designation. I know that might be what other girls want, but not this girl. Not right away. It's too much too young. I know what's expected of me, but I want the unexpected, so after high school I find a full-time job to work instead of a household to run.

I use the pay from that job to put myself through college while missing the party lifestyle of a coed campus because I take classes at night and work during the day. I also turn twenty-one with liquor and without a baby on my hip. When I graduate from college, I designate myself most likely to buck the trend.

Eight years after high school, my first-date kiss becomes my husband. I meet his steady gaze, say "I do" on a Utah mountain, then move to Idaho to start my first TV reporting job. My new husband doesn't move with me. The separated status of our honeymoon phase really throws people. We both have careers, and the best way to maximize the early stages of those careers is to follow opportunity wherever we need to, even if it means living apart for a while.

Shortly after I move to the Gem State, better known for earthy spuds than sparkling jewels, I speak at a university as a newly married graduate. An undergrad asks me how I plan to have babies. I tell her I plan to have babies just like she plans to have babies, but since this is a journalism course not a sex ed course, I won't offer specifics. That's my initial sarcastic response, then I elaborate by encouraging her to realize women are limitless. There's nothing wrong with wanting a career and kids. Men have both. Women can have both, too.

She's in school to find a baby daddy, so I politely remind her that college tuition pays for degrees, not daddies. I don't want to turn off her search for love; I just want to turn on her desire to love herself first. I probably come across as pushy, but it's frustration driving my intention. Finding a baby daddy is significant, but it's not singular, even if that's all I was expected to do, too.

I then go on to tell her and the rest of the class about my life as a working woman who will also one day be a working mom. And hopefully I'll figure out how to enjoy both outside. Sun, moon, stars. Expect it all, I tell the class, male and female alike, but work for it rather than wish for it.

My multiple choices are mine, as they are for many other women in modern-day America. Sure, there's sacrifice and compromise, but not outright rejection of ambition. Historically, that wasn't always the case. Society is a bit slow to catch on, which is why, still today, a woman honestly asks another woman how she plans to have babies and be the boss.

Pretty sure no one ever asked my grandma about doing both. She was a homemaker. Period. It wasn't up for debate. My mother had to work. That wasn't up for debate either. Both women may have wanted something else, but options were out of the question. There's nothing wrong with staying home or working outside the home. Either scenario becomes hard to cope with when it isn't chosen. Living within forced circumstances creates life-altering results. It's the difference between have to and want to.

Truth be told, my grandma, who was a fabulous baker and a talented seamstress, could have fed a whole town and stitched the napkins across every customer's lap, but she didn't. And my mom just wanted to be in the kitchen, instead of in a cubicle, so she had time to make a dinner our whole family would eat together, but we never did.

For both their sakes, and the millions of other ladies limited before me, I expect kids and a career. That's why I move out of state married, but alone.

I like the married part of my life. I like the reporting part of my life, too. But the pay for that reporting is below poverty level, so my husband stays in Utah with a well-paying sales job. We live in separate states the first two years of our marriage by joint decision and it works professionally, but it sucks personally. I mean, honestly, it severely sucks.

I'm a newlywed in a new state with a new job, and my new husband lives in our native state making real money so we can cover rent for two places while I earn a pittance working overtime telling news stories, making mini-movies, and taking pictures.

Pictures like "Power House," and "Freedom," which hangs directly above our black couch. "Freedom" is a rectangular canvas print of a trout mid-ladder. Not a career ladder like the one I'm scrambling up, but a fish ladder. They're placed in rivers to help fish "step" and then rest while swimming a current altered by us in ways that make natural passage no longer possible.

This particular ladder leads to the spawning shed at Henry's Lake, a stocked trophy trout lake in Island Park, Idaho.

I snapped the ladder shot just as a trout jumped another step, its gills flaring, mouth gaping, eyes bulging. The fish is out of water, exposed to danger, but only for the shutter of one fast snapshot. Then it's into the flow of the next step down. The fish is facing the camera, so I know it's on its way out of the spawning shed. It left its seed for the stocking program and now it's back to the lake, back to freedom.

The fish engineered in the shed by man mixing female eggs with male milt (the fish version of sperm) return to the shed because that's what's imprinted on them as their birthplace—just like Utah is my birthplace, even though I call Idaho home.

The fish return so early in the spawning season that the lake is still frozen. They start swimming under the ice toward the shed in February. There's a massive icicle in the right corner of the framed fish on the run on my wall. The shed closes when the fish stop swimming to it in April. The fishery's future finishes fertilizing right about the time the ice melts across the lake.

I rarely fish Henry's Lake. It's more for bait fishermen who want to take home a trophy trout and eat it for dinner. I prefer

to fish with a fly rather than a worm, and I release most of what I catch rather than eat it. That's why I stand in Henry's Fork more often than I boat on Henry's Lake.

I learn to fly-fish Idaho's rivers when I'm not covering stories about crops and crime. I teach my husband how to cast when he visits on weekends. He teaches me how to manage money and keeps me out of debt while I chase my career.

That bold bald eagle from the 1980s, with its inevitably doomed disappearance story, stays with me. Its banana-yellow eyes a flash frame in my mind, my eyes-up reminder: its can't-quit charisma pecking at the backs of besties, the church with its charity, and those who say a shy kid can't be a reporter. I look that TV camera right in the lens, aggressively grab the masses, and say, "I'll show you."

I sign one TV contract after another while moving around the country for news reporting jobs. With every career advancement, I shed more of my quiet self and gain more experience with brutal clarity.

One news director doesn't hire me because my eyes are too close together. Those eyes I'd always looked down with are finally up after twenty-five years, and now they're too close to each other on my face? He tells me people don't want to watch too-close eyes on TV.

Another news director says I'm too white for an on-camera job in Alabama. In the South, people don't watch white girls. Everywhere else, white reporters are a dime a dozen.

Competition is cutthroat. Women don't want me on camera. Men don't want me in their business . . . or in their woods. I want to kick every boy in the balls who says, "You're not a man. We need a man, especially on outdoor assignments. Those aren't for you."

My internal rebuttal continues as the external issues keep trying to morph my being, make me fit. On it goes, me staring eyes-up at shameless scoldings.

You're not trashy enough to cover crime in Vegas. Flip your hair up in the Midwest; it makes you look friendly. Curl it under in the West. That's more conservative. Wear skirts. Wear suits. Wear bright colors because your hair is dull. Wait. Color your hair instead. Don't wear sparkles on your lips because it makes you look like a porn star. Wait, add more sparkles.

And this biting zinger, reaching back from the deep depths of my most buried shy tendencies to haunt me: What's wrong with your voice? Confidence is in your too-close eyes, but authority isn't coming out of your too-quiet mouth. Speak louder. Slower. Deeper. Shoot whiskey before voicing scripts; it relaxes that forced delivery you're struggling with.

I couldn't push my eyes farther apart. I didn't change my gender, either, but I did everything else. All of it with gusto. Shape my shell all you want as long as I can have the career I want. Not want, need. I need to report the truths of the times just like I need to write with my left hand. It's a built-in tendency.

And finally, I'm a messenger for the masses. A lead, live reporter for a decade, moving through every network affiliate but CBS. I didn't avoid CBS—that's just how TV deals shake out sometimes. Same with where you live. You go wherever opportunity shakes out. You live where you work, not vice versa. Make the station your life wherever you end up report-ing because the reality is, you won't play much. And if you do get a day off, you'll be so far from home that trying to cast a fly-fishing rod from the deck of a bass boat in a Kentucky pond will make you the village idiot. Trust me, I know. I tried it once on a steamy July weekend with sweaty hands sticking to fish-ing line and humidity running down my neck, back, and legs.

Total bust on recreation, but reporting . . . reporting I've got despite pitting out every shirt on every live shot.

I'm showing and people are looking, listening, and learning. Millions of them. I'm telling them what's really going on and I'm telling them why it really matters. I'm educating and I'm entertaining.

The scuffle over how I look and how I sound is just reducing distraction. Reducing distraction increases attention. That's what I want: your attention. And I get it every time I tell you a story. Not in a way that centers the content on me; I'm not the story. I want your attention because when I speak of what matters, I want you engaged. It takes a lot to get me to speak, so you better engage when I do.

With every live shot, green screen, set design, teleprompter, camera, and script, I'm telling you that this world of ours hosts magnificent stories, especially natural resource stories, like wolves returning to the West, salmon disappearing from rivers, solar power, wind energy, wildlife migration, urban sprawl, forest access, water rights, drought, flood, and fire.

I don't officially own the outdoor beat—that beat doesn't exist in most media markets—but I want it to. Between covering crops and crime, going live over dead people, staying dead serious during bloopers, and shining despite dull headlines, I push outdoor stories inside TVs, too.

But then I grow tired of pushing. I grow tired of working twice as hard for half the money. And I grow tired of moving my husband across the country and back. He grows tired of TV but doesn't grow tired of me. That's why he's mine; he doesn't let go no matter what. He sees my need to fit for what it is, makes me own the obsession, then tells me to use it to my advantage. He tells me I'll make it when . . . When, not if.

After a decade of TV contracts, I go from stations owning my content to me owning my content. I enter a male-dominated industry when I change my reporting career from general assignment to outdoors, but I don't fester over my minority status. I don't need special treatment and I don't need to burn my bra to be recognized. I just need a rock to stand on when we're throwing flies at fish that won't recognize us as male or female anyway. We're all only human in the wild, and that's enough of a separation from beast.

With my mind made up, and boundaries broken, I start freelancing in 2006. A freelancer in media is like a free agent in sports. All responsibility, respect, and credibility rely on the freelancer—not the corporation. I grow from TV only to all media outlets. My husband grows a beard, and it's more significant to me than I want to admit. When I was little, I couldn't connect with hairy faces, so I put them in the dangerous category, a logical designation for things I didn't know how to trust. I thought beards were for liars and leavers, but my husband doesn't lie and he never leaves. He isn't hiding anything with his beard. He's still as unfiltered as he's always been and we still connect. I love his hairy face as much as I love journalism as a freelancer.

Accepting beards surprises me. And that shy little girl who is now covering stories about a bird that didn't disappear surprises everyone else.

PART II

Chasing

BANDING BALDIES

THREE DECADES AFTER my eagle-eyed experience in the school gym, I'm ankle deep in mud with gray facial hair. Chin and top lip, but not cheek. It's Michael Whitfield, a truth teller regardless of grooming. He's the man who bands bald eagles for research in the Greater Yellowstone Ecosystem (GYE). The GYE includes Yellowstone National Park and Grand Teton National Park plus portions of Idaho, Montana, and Wyoming.

Michael started banding bald eagles right about the same time I was staring at a big bird in Utah. Back then, there were barely a dozen bald eagle pairs nesting along Idaho's South Fork of the Snake River. Now Michael keeps track of more than eighty nests by putting leg bands on baby baldies for tracking purposes. We're on our way to one of the nests he monitors.

It's been thirty years since I saw a bald eagle. Michael is ending my dry spell and proving that wide-brimmed-hat biologist from way back when wrong. He has to intrude to do it. I intrude, too; that's part of my job. If I don't intrude, I don't get the story, so I intrude. Empty-handed is full of hollow.

Eagles don't like intruders. The protective pair we're approaching is raising one eaglet in a nest that older birds built in a giant, ridgeline-high Douglas fir back in the 1980s. The anxious adults circle like desperate vultures and yell like angry parents because we've invaded their space. It's a scene I need to capture, but I must stop working and stare if only for a moment.

The white-headed bird with banana-yellow eyes is circling twenty feet over my head. It's not happy to see me, but I sure do love seeing it. I've grown up from nine and grown out of shy, mostly, and this is the odds-defying bird. Its extended wings and soaring screams are my personal spectacular reward.

"It's a tremendous success story for a lot of people's efforts in managing their habitat and managing the animals," Michael says while I stare fixated on feathers that are surviving in the wild. "This place is incredibly rich in the diversity of flora and fauna."

Michael's work makes for an incredibly rich story. He still sees bald eagles as mysterious. The eaglet he's taking out of a canvas bag carefully lowered from the nest to the ground by a rope is no exception. Its plumage is unusual. Instead

of the common all-black coloring of young bald eagles, the six-week-old bird is speckled black and white. Its talons also toggle between black and white. Michael quickly records the first feather variation discovered at Palisades Reservoir.

"I'm entranced. The more I watch bald eagles, the more mystery there is," he says, wrapping the bird's talons around his fingers.

The South Fork of the Snake River flows out of Palisades Reservoir. The sixty-six-mile stretch is stunning even though it no longer has a natural starting point. The South Fork starts where the Snake River is clogged for agriculture in a big tub, the reservoir. The reservoir is ringed by a thick forest of evergreens with a plug of cement at the northern end. The Snake stops flowing freely behind the man-made dam, backs up the bath to the fill line, then is released in rations during irrigation season to water the growth of potatoes and grain. Yes, South Fork flows are controlled like so many other western waters, but it's still stunning and it's still surviving in a state of untamed the farther you float from the dam.

Miraculously, the canyon stretch, where bald and golden eagles eye you, is largely undeveloped with two *P*-word priorities I sleep better knowing exist: public and protected. There's very little private land in the canyon, which means it's open to the public. And large tracts of land are protected through conservation easements. Easements ensure the land isn't developed long into the future.

The South Fork also hosts the largest cottonwood tree gallery in the West. The moose here are huge, and so are the deer. They have to be. Winters are brutal in the canyon, followed by spring flows that scare the best oarsmen.

Even when eagles were scarce, they were still screaming on the South Fork. It's a stronghold for baldies in the West, and Michael has banded hundreds of them over the years. He's still following birds he banded more than twenty years ago. Now he has a color morph to follow as he bands the bird's leg and tucks it carefully back into the bag for a rope ride up the tree. My eyes, and my lens, follow his every move.

"Every nest I've been in has a magnificent view," he says, pulling rope while watching the bag rise. "Eagles pick the biggest structure that's available. They pick a high place where they can see a long ways. You get a whole different perspective of the world from an eagle nest."

I'd like to see that, but I won't get to. The anxious adults are returning. They think they've won. They've raised enough of a ruckus to run off the humans. In a way, they're right. Now that the eaglet is banded, the humans won't be back. They'll track from afar while the wild does its thing, as it should be free to do.

"People recognize the bald eagle for the majesty that it is," Michael says as we hike away from the nest site. "The fact that it's our national symbol isn't an accident. Bald eagles are symbols of the wildness of this place. I think we need to do all we can to sustain this resource."

Bald eagles successfully flew away from the endangered species list in 2007, with Michael still following their progress. The rare raptor I once saw as a little girl is the same type of bird I now see nearly every day.

I'm an outdoor journalist, born the same year as the endangered species list. I still pick grass out of my shoes. I still study your every move and you still don't know it.

ILLEGAL EAGLES

I'M GUARDING TWENTY thousand dollars' worth of camera equipment on the pickup curb at Denver International Airport. I'm wearing a vest instead of a coat because the weather is mild. Summer is close. I smell it in the warm ground straddling the runways. There's a four-door sedan with its windows rolled down idling at the curb. The driver gets out because I'm not getting in. I'm wide-eyed with panic, hearing my mother in my head.

"Don't talk to strangers," she's saying with worry wrinkles around her eyes. *"And certainly don't get in their cars. Not even for a story."*

Talking to and getting in are what I do on a daily basis. When I'm on assignment, I have to develop instant rapport with strange people in strange places. For a girl who grew up painfully shy, this is a taxing development later in life, but I do it daily.

The reason I hear my mother during this particular pickup is because of what I see on the driver and in his back seat. He's packing heat, a handgun holstered on his hip, and his car is stocked with survival supplies. It's not as shocking as the cabbie who picked me up in the South Carolina swamps, shoeless and with his pants undone, but it's alarming nonetheless.

"Welcome to Denver," says my clean-shaven Colorado contact. "We've got a bit of a drive and only a few hours to get this done, so what are you waiting for?"

I'm waiting for reassurance. I need more than smooth cheeks. I look him up and down. He works out, but I run far. Drive me out to the boonies with mischief in mind and I'll make a mad dash back to the city. Endurance trail running for 50Ks isn't just for exercise. Mental plan in place, I get in the car. My driver is a federal agent. He's supposed to be the good guy anyway. That's the other reason I get in his car.

EarthFix, a division of PBS, commissioned me to do a story on illegal eagle trade, and the project led me here, to the National Eagle Repository and the National Wildlife Property Repository, outside of Denver, Colorado. That's where U.S. Fish and Wildlife Service (FWS) stores evidence from trafficking cases after the judicial proceedings conclude, and that's where my driver, Dan Rolince, is taking me. He's the assistant

special agent in charge of the U.S. Fish and Wildlife Service Office of Law Enforcement. Most of the agents he supervises are undercover, but he's not. That's why I can interview him on camera. He talks about hard-to-trace cases on the drive.

"Making a wildlife case is extremely difficult," he says. "Typically the victim does not have the opportunity to call you and tell you something happened."

That sounds awful and looks worse. We arrive at the warehouse, and my worry over becoming Dan's next victim is forgotten. I'm surrounded by dead animals. It's overwhelming. My eyes won't fix on any one item: gorilla hands here, tiger heads there, seahorses on lower shelves, and those once-endangered eagles up higher.

The display is massive and gruesome, the effects of wildlife trafficking. I can't help but gape jaw-dropped at the morbid creations before clearing my head of sorrow and capturing the horrific and uncomfortable scene with my video camera.

I look around via lens: snake wine, antelope scarves, and bins and bins of elephant tusks, crushed as if Grandma's china cabinet toppled. But the ivory didn't arrive at the warehouse like this—FWS destroyed it. In 2013, the service pummeled six tons of ivory with an industrial rock crusher, and now the bins join the repository's more than one-million-piece evidence collection. A show of no tolerance for trafficking by making the ivory worthless.

The repository opened in the 1980s, and some items have been here since the beginning, but the collection continues to grow. Coolers filled with eagles show up the day I arrive. After bald and golden eagles—dead of natural causes or killed illegally—arrive, FWS distributes the feathers, talons, wings, and other parts to Native American tribes, who use them for ceremonies and religious services. While the eagles are repurposed, almost nothing else leaves the shelves of this museum-like warehouse.

Two hours later I finish filming and wander the aisles without working. I'm disturbingly fascinated by the strange spectacles that once roamed the wild. But at the same time, what I see makes me feel sick, and I'm not alone in that emotional response. Dan is as somber as a mortician, giving me a few minutes of silence to absorb the kind of disgusting you want to look away from, but you can't.

The collection is the result of two hundred agents working wildlife cases nationwide, with an additional two hundred inspectors at ports of entry into the United States. I hate the whole thing. It doesn't fit. It shouldn't fit. And it hurts. Humanity's black eye.

I come upon items made from animals that inhabit the West, my longtime home: eagle talons, elk antlers, deer hides. I don't want to see them here in this condition, crowded on these shelves, far removed from their natural state. I hate that they were illegally traded, but at least this is not my first impression of them. I've seen these creatures alive and in abundance in the wild. The bald eagles that didn't disappear fly over my house daily.

But I haven't seen a wild elephant in person. I'm drawn to the section that houses their remains. Their huge feet double as flower pots, footrests, and waste baskets. There's a pile of elephant-hair bracelets and a stack of hides. Among the stash, I spot two tusks, carved delicately into the shapes of a man and a woman, leaning lovingly toward each other. How hands of such harm can create such beauty escapes me.

I study the intricate carvings closely, then notice what is propped on the wall behind them: a large elephant skin cut into the shape of Africa. Across it, it bears a painting of an elephant in motion, its ears fanned widely. I would find such a sight in the wild amazing, and I hope to witness it one day—but, staring at an animal painted on its own skin, I fear I may never have the opportunity. That's a painful realization, but this is the reality of wildlife trafficking, packed into a repository in the outskirts of Denver.

Through my now warehouse-weary eyes, Dan is a hero. I don't hesitate to ride with him back to the airport. I'm more worried about the poachers he's after than him. A warehouse full of atrocities changes your perspective that fast.

SEEKING REFUGE

THE UNEASE I felt when I first met agent Dan with a gun on his hip is nothing compared to the guns on hips I'm focused on now, most of them belonging to patchy beards.

My lens is obvious and wide-open, hot with criminal curiosity. My hands, hidden in my pockets, are fisted, closed with cold confusion.

So much of this news-breaking scene seems staged. Most of it, in fact. Except for the guns. The guns are real and loaded—fire-at-will mentality with that will coming from a militia making a statement on public lands as its New Year's resolution.

I'm covering the standoff at Malheur National Wildlife Refuge in Oregon. I arrived at this hostile situation on the sunny heels of a friendly assignment in Florida.

Ironically, I couldn't see the landscape when I arrived in the Sunshine State. It was dark, the power knocked out, completely dropping the curtain on Florida's Sanibel Island. I could only hear the ocean rolling in the licorice-colored night.

A week later, here I am in Oregon, where my eyes don't lock on landscape again. The refuge is smothered in white fog as thick as marshmallow cream. I can only hear cattle calling in the heavy mist.

Limited landscape visibility is the only thing these two refuges have in common during my first visit to both.

Florida's Gulf Coast caters to the wild. On Sanibel Island, no building can be higher than a palm tree. You must slow down for swooping owls, and it's lights-out for nesting turtles at night. Seventy percent of the region is protected in its natural state. The mangrove majesty of J.N. Ding Darling National Wildlife Refuge, at 6,400 acres, is included in that protection. Developing it, or changing it in any way, isn't debated in this community.

Randall Marsh is part of that community. He's a sunbaked and thinly bearded fishing guide with more than two professional decades on the water. Tarpon are his preferred target, but I'm on his boat in January and it's too cold for tarpon. Apparently it's too cold for Randall, too. I'm barefoot and he looks bundled to plow snow. We compare fish stories of the salt-

and freshwater varieties, recognizing we fish for both on public land.

"People want to see this," Randall says while slowly sliding past mangroves. "People want to come see a Florida that's not high-rises and Disney World."

Malheur National Wildlife Refuge (NWR) in Oregon's Harney Basin is far from Disney World, but there's still plenty of action on its undeveloped acres, especially right now. When I arrive, I'm so fresh off the beach that the itch of coastal bug bites on my inland-bred shoulders flares as my camera pack settles on my back.

I orient myself in the fog by finding the watchtower at refuge headquarters. Below the tower, there's a heap of heated bodies carefully duckwalking across an icy lot to make a statement in front of a line of cameras. Their unsteady steps on the slick surface discount the seriousness of the gunslinging situation. But once they plant their feet around the mic, hike up their holstered jeans, and puff out their proud chests, there's no doubting their intent.

They're not here for a friendly game of pond hockey. They're here to claim this place as theirs. The problem is, the land they want for themselves is public land, so it also belongs to everyone else. That's the brilliance behind our nation's public land. Taking away our access to Malheur to claim it as their own goes against the exact reason we're all gathering here on land we all own. It's confounding.

It's also cold. I'm trying to keep my fingers from freezing while also trying to get a grip on my drastic change in circumstance. Gone are the mangroves. No more sun and no more unquestioned devotion to public land. I must change modes in a hurry and the adjustment is rough. History is unfolding in front of me, and it's not waiting for my sun-soaked body to recover.

My discomfort rolls to the back of my mind as I focus on the uncomfortable challenge before me. I need to hear from both sides. To do that, I don't hang with who seems the sanest or the safest and I don't start talking right away. I unload my gear without saying a word and listen to the conversations going on around me.

When I first started shedding my shy self, I talked all the time. I thought I had to fill the silence so someone wouldn't suspect me of being too afraid to speak. That tactic doesn't lead to usable interviews. Listening, without interrupting, creates solid comments within an interview. It's okay to draw emotion out by asking hard questions, but don't ask those questions mid-quote. It ruins the speaker's train of thought and it's rude. Being rude to someone who agrees to be interviewed leaves you with no interview.

I ruined stories when I started reporting because I overused my newfound voice when what I really wanted was the person being interviewed to speak. I went from not being enough for myself to being too much for everyone else, and that weakened my assignments. Seeing, and hearing, my blunders frame by frame in the edit bay in the early days of my career taught me a lesson in a hurry. Stories are better when you listen and best when you listen to both sides.

My priority at Malheur is capturing both sides of this dynamic story in raw form, unedited sight and uncensored sound. That's what I gather while studying the strangers around me and the strange land we're all standing on.

Malheur NWR is 187,757 acres of undeveloped country set aside for wildlife. It's a broad landscape of shallow sagebrush in the middle of cow country. It's also in the middle of a standoff, which is why it's closed now. A group calling themselves the Citizens for Constitutional Freedom took over the refuge shortly after the ball dropped on New Year's Eve 2016. They claim the government is overextending its reach by limiting ranchers and their grazing practices on public land. They cut federal fencing at the refuge and added a gate, saying the land belonged to a rancher who had been shut out. Now we're all shut out as people fight over who gets to use the land and how.

That's why I'm here. It's my job to cover what's going on outside, and that doesn't always mean fun topics like a warm fishing trip in Florida. From covering stories about water wars and wildfires to fights over access and rights, I witness the failures, the struggles, and the triumphs that unfold on public land among the bearded and beardless alike. I know well not to judge a face by its hair anymore. The cleanest ones can be the dirtiest.

Not far from the compelling face-to-face showdown with a mob of media circling wagons around it, I see a pheasant and quietly back away from the crowd with my camera. My earpiece is still wirelessly connected to the mic I left in the huddle. It's an odd sensation to have a wild saga playing in your ear while the real wild struts in front of your eyes, oblivious to the human struggle across the ditch.

The rooster is native, not stocked by man. I can tell by the spurs on its legs. Pen-raised pheasants are often clipped of spurs. I stay hidden in the fringe as the upland bird with long, colorful tail feathers brushes its way across a flat, snow-covered field like a painter's first stroke on clean canvas. Its clawed feet are an X-marks-the-spot chain tracking across the white as the paintbrush slides away.

I know the occupiers have guards with guns and they have me in their sights, but I keep the pheasant in mine and keep rolling. Shooting the camerawoman while tape records won't do any of them any good. That's what I tell my nervous self while painting bravery on my own canvas.

My confidence bolsters a notch when the pheasant's cocked walk unintentionally mimics the puffed-chest men my lens just left. That's funny stuff, so I smile, settling into the scene. When a coyote yips, I laugh out loud. Its cries are louder than the men yelling. Nature is going about its business regardless of who is sitting in the refuge watchtower. And so am I.

There are more than 560 NWRs in the United States. Every state has at least one. I have seven in Idaho. Randall has twenty-nine in Florida, but really we all have access to every NWR regardless of where we live, what we do, or how much money we make. No standoff gets to undo that.

Watching a heated exchange at refuge headquarters is almost as fascinating as watching brown trout hunt or grizzly bears swim. But given the choice, I choose browns and bears over a pissing match any day.

PRESENCE LOST

I'M IN A hotel room in Galveston, Texas, a few months after Malheur. A thunderstorm is keeping me from saltwater snapper fishing, but I'm entertained anyway. I'm holding a book published in 1907 titled *The Use of the National Forests*.

I've decided to read the whole book in one night based on its enticing introduction:

"TO THE PUBLIC. Many people do not know what National Forests are. Others may have heard much about them, but have no idea of their true purpose and use. A little misunderstanding may cause a great deal of dissatisfaction."

How true those words ring today. I bet that's why Jim Caswell brought the book from his home state of Idaho, public lands percentage 62, to Texas, public lands percentage 2. Jim is well groomed and well spoken. He's the Bureau of Land Management's former national director. He's also the Clearwater National Forest's former forest supervisor. He knows plenty more than a thing or two about public lands. He held the little old red book in one hand and a big newer green book in the other hand during his keynote dinner speech and said:

"This is why we are where we are today. We've lost perspective. We've lost the people."

Jim's comments speak volumes and so do his props. The skinny red one is forty-two pages. The fat green one, *The Principal Laws Relating to Forest Service Activities*, published in 1993, is 1,163 pages. Jim loaned me both for the night, but I only plan on reading one. The thick binding keeps me from cracking the cover on the green book, but I wholeheartedly eyeball the red read, its pages so old, they smell like wisdom edged with worn exposure. The red book is the why behind the establishment of public lands where I live.

The West as I know it is wild by origin, bearded by nature, and unfit for mainstream. Just like me, I'm finding out.

Public lands are part of me personally and professionally. Public lands, managed by the government for the people, are where I play. Public lands are also where I work. I've always been aware of public lands, and I value them with sincere gratitude. They are my place, where I fit naturally. They are the one certainty this western girl knew would never expire.

"I said, 'It will never happen,' for a long time, but now I'm not so sure," Jim says while still holding the books high. "Will it go anywhere? I'm not sure."

As more public land is traded for and transferred to private, I'm not so sure either, and I should have seen the warning signs during my first TV contract as a general assignment reporter. I clearly remember covering the closure of the U.S. Forest Service office in St. Anthony, Idaho, population 3,342 in 2000.

The logging town was already declining when the feds combined the Caribou and Targhee National Forests. Rural offices closed, including the one in St. Anthony, and staff consolidated in the central location of Idaho Falls. Idaho Falls is small by city definition, but much larger than the farm and timber town forty-five minutes north.

Green trucks and brown uniforms disappeared in St. Anthony, and so did jobs and people. St. Anthony had seventy-one full-time Forest Service positions before consolidation. That staff went from being local neighbors you chatted with at the grocery store to employees in a big-city building down south where you waited in the lobby to possibly talk with the guy you used to bump shopping carts with on aisle 12.

The closure story I covered in Idaho mirrored closures and consolidations across the country. Federal budgets were drying up long before states started volleying for land transfers. I knew the money was going away, but what I didn't pick up on back then was what those closures meant to communities beyond jobs. Sure, it meant payroll lost, but it also meant presence lost.

"We've lost our public support. We've lost our constituency," Jim says. "People do not go to battle for us anymore. They've lost confidence in us and rightly so in many cases."

Presence lost doesn't have to be permanent. Not if Garth Smelser has anything to do with it. He served as forest supervisor for the Caribou-Targhee National Forest from 2014 to

2017. He's post-consolidation and he's young by agency standards. He didn't have to ride out the relocation saga at the turn of this century, and he never lived in St. Anthony. The Idaho Falls location is all he knows, but he's aware of presence lost.

"Presence has to be the most important thing. Through increased presence, we gain greater understanding. Understanding brings relevance, which leads to advocacy," Garth says during one of our many discussions about public lands. "We do have that danger of losing a generation that even cares. If we don't help them learn to love public land, why should we expect them to take care of it?"

I don't run into Garth at the grocery store, but we talk. We talk about our little kids loving the outdoors. We talk about getting everyone's kids outside. Those are personal, friendly talks. We also talk about permits and about presence. Those are professional talks, and they can get heated but end productively.

"Presence is key to many agency problems," he says. "It is the realization that we live here, too. If I can be present with people in my uniform having a civil and respectful conversation, I create dividends that I don't even know are coming down the road. Even over contentious issues, they'll remember I cared about their opinions."

Garth wants the presence of public lands back and so do I. Jim wants it back, too. Without presence, public lands lose relevance. Public lands lose priority. Without presence and without priority, there is no reason to fight for something no one is paying attention to.

Jim had me paying attention, and I wanted others paying attention, so I frantically scribbled story notes in my old-school reporter's notebook while he spoke during dinner. A reporter's notebook is a narrow spiral of lined paper that fits in your palm, like the pad your order is written on at a restaurant. I can type notes faster on my phone, but I think that looks like I've checked out to text idle comments that end with emojis instead of periods. I'm far from checked out when I'm on a story, so I stick to writing notes that also look like I'm listening.

With straight posture and scooted to the edge of my seat in the front row, I can feel the end of any speech coming. I can sense it in a well-versed speaker's demeanor and the space between us. It's like the slight pause of anticipation in a fireworks show right before the grand finale. That pause is my cue to put the pen in my left hand to the paper in my right and dictate word for word what is said.

Jim's slight pause, my cue, was the lowering of his two props. He set them down on the podium and looked at the crowd, delivering not a punch line but rather a punch to the gut. His words as thick as the green book bulging with regulation and as short on beating around the bush as the skinny red one.

"If we lose our public land heritage, we've lost a lot for a long, long time," Jim said, tapping each hand to a book. "Yeah, there are some rules and you need to be a responsible adult, but by and large, it's open and you can do what you want. For that reason, we have to protect public lands. We have to keep them public. They are worth fighting for."

LONE WOMAN
IN WHITE

A FEW MONTHS after meeting Jim and reading that red book, I'm in my home state for my fifteenth wedding anniversary, but I'm not home. I'm laying fly line on Idaho's East Fork of the Salmon River at sunset. I help cook dinner on my truck's tailgate turned table. I mingle with every man in camp but my husband. He's not here.

I'm on the road with Idaho Public Television. We're heading into the White Cloud Mountains to shoot scenics from every route, angle, and way possible for a new *Outdoor Idaho* episode. The mountain range is about to shift from forest designation to wilderness, giving this public land an added layer of pristine protection. The designation is decades in the making, and it's no easy feat given the current debate over subtracting public land versus adding it.

I've never seen the White Clouds and I want to. I'll admit, being here without my husband is not exactly the anniversary I had in mind, but it will have to do this year. We are secure in our marriage, unlike my parents' on-and-off effort when I was younger.

When *Outdoor Idaho* producer John Crancer called with the invite, I couldn't say yes fast enough. I rattled off my strengths to prove myself a crew asset: I'm running a wilderness race in that area; I'm rafting the Middle Fork of the Salmon River and chasing fish close by; I'm in shape and carry my fair share of work weight; I know how to shoot with five different cameras. John liked what he heard. My husband didn't, but he gets it.

We married following the burst of a fierce thunderstorm in July 1999. The ceremony was on a peak in Utah's Wasatch Mountains, and the photos turned out perfect after the rain stopped, but we rarely recognize the wedding date in the summer. We usually celebrate our anniversary in the winter, because summer is peak shooting season for me and my production schedule is always in the way. This is one of the many quirks of my career that my husband tolerates.

He's a beautiful man in all the ways a human should be. He's as strong as a bear, but lean and fit. I've never seen anyone hotter in the woods. This is confirmed by the list of contacts

photo credit: Aaron Kunz

in my phone. Sometime during my heavily medicated state of broken leg recovery, I changed his name to "Hotness." Imagine my surprise when I started receiving texts from Hotness, having no memory of making the change. In my eyes, no one I work with even comes close to his kind of handsome. What makes him even more so is his heartfelt understanding of what I need even when I don't know what that is myself.

Shortly after I started freelancing, the Great Recession hit. My husband was upper management at a large corporation, and the uppers lost their jobs first. I told him I had us covered and wouldn't let us down. He knew I was sincere, so we pulled our boys out of daycare and he stayed home with them while I traveled for work.

Despite our parents' discomfort with our nontraditional home life, it went well for a few years until my work started waning and our savings started shrinking. Our household had a delayed reaction to the recession because we didn't have any debt, but at a certain point, most Americans needed more than debt-free status to make it during the recession.

I panicked and turned desperate, making decisions that weren't smart, like working for less money because less was still more than none. I didn't like myself or our situation, even though other families were floundering just like we were. I'm ashamed to say this, but I was overdosing on mental mutilation and beating myself hard for my shortcomings. In other words, I was handling myself in a disrespectful manner. That's when my husband stepped in, and all these years later I still remember the intensity of his lecture.

We were walking the block midweek in the middle of the day. When I move, my mouth moves, so I was spouting as we progressed through the neighborhood. I was crying because I didn't have us. I wasn't working hard enough or fast enough. I wasn't enough to keep us going. I thought I was failing us.

I continued ranting and berating myself with eastern Idaho's notorious cold spring wind blasting my face and encouraging snot and more tears. My husband listened for a long time, as he's known to do, then he stopped walking. He spun me toward him and got right in my face, the heat of his anger in stark contrast to the chill in the air.

"It breaks my heart when you break your own spirit," he said. "My goal in life is to see you happy and when you're not, I am failing. You succeed one hundred times for every one failure, and you never remember that. Never. But I do and I'm reminding you now. You've done all you can in our current situation. We both have. Now leave yourself alone or I will leave you alone until you do."

He didn't leave, but he got through to me. I hear that speech in my head every time I'm too ugly with myself. The last thing my husband wants to do is hold me back, but the last thing he's going to let me do is beat myself up.

He also knows it's best to let me run free when he'd rather keep me close to his side. Smothering me in concern doesn't guarantee safety or survival. Smarts and skills in tough conditions do that. I use both in the tough conditions offered in the White Clouds where I'm working with the public TV crew.

The first few miles are treeless and steep. It's hostile among dusty brown hills with insects buzzing while I'm baking in the sun. I quickly realize that the White Clouds want to kick the endurance right out of you. The elevation, the distance, the bugs. All three try my patience, but I don't give in. Following my dad in his well-intentioned but often misguided footsteps—his refusal to admit when he's lost has taught me not to.

The terrain changes at about mile four. It's still hot and buggy, but pine trees start shading our trek and the ground is meadow green instead of desert brown. I'm studying the changes in the landscape when I spot the Cloud's crown jewel—Castle

Peak pushing almost twelve thousand feet in elevation. It's a sight that shouts, "This is why you don't turn around early and you never quit."

Castle Peak looks like home. My native home, where the Wasatch Mountains dominate the skyline like Castle does here. In my native home, Mormons organized Salt Lake City in an orderly square-block grid. It's an efficient design, a design I understand even if the doctrine leans too religiously heavy for me. I'd rather pray in the forest than in the front pew. The weekly ritual of inside sacrament is not my thing, but their streets I get.

They're sequentially numbered and easy to navigate, counting higher from Main Street to the Wasatch in the east and the Oquirrhs in the west. The church's temple, Temple Square, is ground zero for the street-numbering system running north and south. Choose a number east or west, then a number north or south, and you have the coordinates for a particular spot on the grid. You'll find your place.

Castle Peak holds its place and doesn't make you look for it. It doesn't sidle up on you with a shy introduction, either. It shoots out of the ground with a look-at-me presence. There's no way you can look away. Same effect with the Wasatch, the peaks that formed the playground of my youth, the same peaks I married on. The trunky tug on my heart pulls instantly. I wouldn't trade the Castle for the Wasatch, but I like seeing peaks that look like home. That's a comforting feeling when you're the lone woman on the White Clouds crew.

Most of the men I work with hunt and fish, or hike and bike, and that's the talk around the campfire at the end of the day, but the *Outdoor Idaho* crew talks of more. We all enjoy the outdoors in various forms, and tall tales run rapid through base camp, but we're also lens lovers. We see the world as frames of visual perfection. I constantly view my surroundings in frame mode, looking at scenes from the angle that best fills the lens even when I'm not holding a camera. Others on the *OI* crew do the same. We compare tips and tricks, bold moves and bumbles. That's our fireside chat until it rains and we all run for cover.

I'm seven unlit miles from the trailhead. There's no easy out, so I give myself a pep talk and crawl inside my one-man, or rather my no-man, tent. There are no men in my tent. I'm alone and in the dark, and I'm lonely. I'm thinking of home as I slowly prepare for a solo sleep in the suffocating dark. I don't like the dark. I don't like it at all. My camera doesn't work in the dark. I'm blind to what's coming at me in the dark. Beard? Or beardless? There's no telling void of light.

The woods are wet-tar dark and I'm swimming in lonely anxiety because I'm afraid of the dark. This overnighter is a cruel experiment testing my brawn. Will I stay the night or bail by walking back to the trailhead, convinced that moving through the dark is better than lying in it? If I can make it until morning, I can tell myself the dark doesn't scare me anymore.

Mother Nature must know I'm wavering, so she distracts me with a twelve-hour thunderstorm. Lightning illuminates the fabric walls of my tent, rain pours, hail piles, but I'm dry with eyes unseeing, limbs unmoving, until the White Clouds and its Castle come calling at daybreak. Better yet, I stayed. I enjoy the sprout of my solo bravery as the sun rises. I disguise that personal success as professional excitement when I inspect my camera cases and find that they are indeed waterproof and leak proof.

We all emerge from our soggy tents with bed head and bad breath. The bed head stays. The bad breath is brushed away as talk of the day brews with the coffee. Mine is the only face in camp that hasn't grown hair overnight.

In true shooter fashion, we're all grateful it rained during dark hours. A downpour during daylight shooting hours is heartbreaking. We have no rain when the sun comes up. The filming festival in the White Clouds is glistening with potential.

We divide into three teams and go our separate ways for the day. I climb closer to Castle Peak to shoot aerial footage in a meadow. Along the way, I mentally wish my husband a happy anniversary and decide we should spend an anniversary in the White Clouds together. He lightens the dark and he needs to see peaks that look like home, too.

GREEN WITH ENVY

I'M A SWINGER. I have to be. The man in wire-rimmed glasses, making him look irritated rather than educated, is sure of it. He's loafing around by the drinking fountain in the baggage claim area. He's watching luggage spin and he's listening to Chris Hunt. I've spent many miles on the water with Chris. Him pretending to catch a fish. Me pretending to make a movie.

I've adjusted my settings from one manly crew of seven in the White Clouds to one man with the stature of seven in the Idaho Falls Regional Airport.

We're an uncanny couple when we travel together for work. Our size difference is stunning. I'm a hobbit. He's a yeti. Stick us in a drift boat with me in the front and I look like a toddler dangling on the high end of a teeter-totter. Chris is a staffer with Trout Unlimited's media team and he has more height and weight than me, but I have more hair. Regardless, his stature draws attention, especially when he opens his mouth, which he does as soon as my husband, Hotness, walks into the airport to pick me up.

"Thanks for sharing your wife with us," Chris says.

It's not the first time my husband's heard that, but definitely a first for shocked guy-in-glasses now spitting water back into the drinking fountain. His kind of share is not our kind of share, but we let his mind wander because that kind of confusion is knee-slappingly funny.

My husband doesn't miss a beat and asks if we caught anything. I tell him I caught, lost, and caught again. He wants all of the details to make sense of my cryptic answer, so I indulge him.

I'm producing my first film for Trout Unlimited. It's about Utah's stretch of the Green River. The Green is a marvelous ribbon of blue water wrapping around red rock. I need to study its flow because there's a pipeline proposal floating to the surface. If approved, it would move the Green across the Continental Divide to water Denver.

I'm documenting what the Green looks like pre-pipe in 2011. I'm also researching how a pipeline would change that look and exploring just how deep this river runs in the West's

photo credit: Charlie Card

veins. It doesn't take me long to find depth. It's in the strong strokes of Charlie Card.

"Take three seconds to look around at where you are," he says while navigating his drift boat with wooden oars. "This is pretty good."

I once had a Colorado fishing guide humiliate me by suggesting that I spend the day in his lap, as that would provide the best angle for my story, in his opinion. Of course he was wrong, in my opinion. I knew that without getting anywhere near the space between his oars.

Charlie is not that guy, far from it. He's the Green's gentleman. His face eternally holds so much youth, I doubt it grows a single whisker. Charlie doesn't cuss and he doesn't drink, but the rest of the crew on this video shoot does. I hear pukers in our community bathroom on early mornings after late nights. As the only female crew member, I always get my own room, but not always my own toilet. Honestly, sharing a bedroom might be easier than sharing a bathroom.

In contrast, time in Charlie's boat is charming. He's the type of fly fishing guide that's so tied up in trout and what they'll take that I know for certain he doesn't want me in his lap any more than I want to sit there. Gender awareness is void between us, and I'm content to wrap myself in my cameras, including the new underwater one I'm learning to manipulate.

I started with one standard definition (SD) video camera in 2006, then upgraded to high-definition (HD) in 2009. That was one year too late. I missed an opportunity to shoot for *National Geographic* because I didn't have an HD camera in 2008. I dragged my feet on the expense only to my detriment. Because of that disadvantage, I jumped early in the movement to 4K (four times the resolution of HD) and underwater and aerial. I wouldn't be left behind again.

I'm a certified drone pilot, which is not an easy test to pass. It's more suited for pilots than producers, but I want every angle I can get and I want overhead shots just as much as I want underwater ones. I sweat when doing both. Truthfully, it's a mind-over-matter miracle that I end up with any usable footage, but I make sure I do.

Shooting footage from a plane makes me motion sick if the flight is longer than ten minutes. Popping pills to level my equilibrium and my line of sight is a must; so is a barf bag. I'm not much calmer on the ground running a drone via remote control, but it's nerves, not motion, causing the problem then. Watching your flying camera nose-dive into the ground like an iron horseshoe drawn to the world's largest magnet turns your stomach. So does drowning one. That's what happens with Charlie.

Charlie, polite as he is, doesn't hesitate to point out one particular fish eluding me.

"I think that was actually the middle fin he flipped you there," he jokes.

Charlie smiles a lot. He has a full smile and a hearty laugh that escapes the space between his two front teeth. As he grins, he rows a calm and constant rhythm that holds its own tune. You can't help but rock to it whether you're casting to fish or capturing footage. It's obvious Charlie doesn't just love the Green. He lives the Green. He's on it more days of the year than he's off it. He doesn't feel right without his regular dose of water. I get that. I don't feel right without my regular dose of fresh air, outside air.

Walt Gasson is the same way, but he drifted farther into Wyoming in his later years. He's Trout Unlimited's director of Endorsed Business, so he doesn't get to put his hands in the Green as often as Charlie does, but he's still anchored by it.

When I'm not on the water with Charlie for this film project, I'm in the sagebrush with Walt.

"The Green River is the sort of place where we go to get our boots dirty and our souls clean," Walt says while rubbing a stem of sage between his thumb and index finger. "It's hard for us to tell where the land leaves off and we begin. Where the river leaves off and we begin."

Three decades separate Charlie and Walt, but they are of the same mind when it comes to the Green.

"If there's one thing that's been constant through the history of the interior West, it's been bad decisions about water," Walt says, releasing the sage and adjusting his cowboy hat. "But this isn't just about water. This is about home. And people will do things for home that they won't do for anything else. I can't stand by and watch our home place be lost."

His home place is spectacular, and by summer's end I've made four trips to the Green. Interviews are done and scenics are in the can. I just need a bit more fish porn, beautiful shots of trout in their natural habitat, underwater. That's all Charlie and I are after as we float the river in September.

Long before selfie sticks, I invented one out of necessity. I need to see what's under Charlie's boat, so I use a trekking pole with a waterproof camera anchored close to its rubber-grip base. My new underwater contraption reveals a world we've been blind to until now. In a system with an estimated fifteen thousand fish per mile, there's no doubt my footage is fishy, but on day three of the shoot, all my footage goes overboard.

I didn't have enough overnight hours between shooting days to dump video files to an external storage drive. Three days of irreplaceable money shots are on the camera that's slipping out of my hands and into the water. I hover between losing my dignity and losing my lunch as I watch the camera sink then roll along the river bottom. Damn the Green for being so clear. I witness every ding, dent, and punch to my lens. It's torture.

The other problem causing panic? The day is hot enough to pool sweat in my breathable waders, but the Green's water heater never works. I'm not a strong enough swimmer to survive the cold and the current, but Charlie is. He strips from the waist up and promises one retrieve attempt. He's modest, so I promise not to shoot any footage of his bare chest if he'll just dive in right now. He does. I hold my breath.

The drowning camera is recording the whole time, and watching it later proves just how well Charlie swims. Not that I care about technique when I first see his hand, holding my camera, surface. Then he emerges. You see me grab for the camera and leave Charlie bobbing in the waves. Chris loves that part. Like his joke about sharing me, Chris never tires of watching the overboard fiasco caught on my own camera.

To this day, the footage still makes me anxious. Charlie still squirms when he watches it, too. In his pale-colored pants, he looks naked. Not exactly the kind of fish porn we were going for, but we laugh about it every time we fish together.

When I head his way these days, I leave my cameras at home and take my husband instead. We've spent many wedding anniversaries in Charlie's boat. My easygoing guy enjoys the floating, the fishing, and the friendly banter every time. And he never worries about sharing his wife.

COLLARING THE WILD

"YES! DID YOU get that?"

"Get what?"

"That deer."

"What deer?"

"The one in the net."

"Where?" I say, lifting my head.

"Put your head down. The deer can't see you."

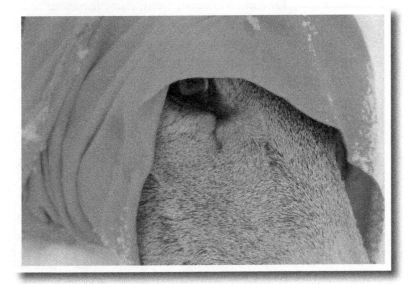

"But if the deer can't see me, I can't see them."

"Shh. Coming in hot on our right."

We hear the sound of a net snapping to my right.

"Oh, he's in good. You got that, right?"

"Got what?"

"That deer tangled in the net on our right."

"Really?" I rise to my knees.

"Stop moving. Stay down. Here comes another one."

This is how a chaotic winter day in the desert goes. The odds of pulling off this story are steep, but I won't back down from the challenge—the challenge of filming deer capture without a tripod, without standing, and, for most of the time, without looking. It sounds ridiculous, but stick me outside, issue the impossible, and I'll go for ridiculous because I know the story will be worth it. I won't settle for less. That's why I chase biologists. They do cool work that turns into even cooler stories, the kind of stories people pay attention to.

Biologist Curtis Hendricks is captain on this mission. He's a regional wildlife manager for the Idaho Department of Fish and Game. I've shot outdoor stories with him for more than a decade. We've spied on pheasants, climbed after sheep, and tackled deer. That's today's chore: tackling deer in a snowstorm and attaching traceable collars.

Curtis is in the "ship." That's the helicopter hovering over our heads, rustling snow in swirls, reducing our visibility to zero. Even if visibility were decent, I wouldn't be allowed to raise my head higher than the sagebrush—Dan Garren is making sure of that. He's the guy giving me the play-by-play while holding my nose to the ground and expecting me to still get footage.

I've known Dan as long as I've known Curtis, and he's been hairy the whole time, very hairy. I've never seen him with his shirt off, but I suspect the growth goes well beyond his goatee.

I've spent such long days with him, I've watched his cheeks go from freshly shaven at sunrise to filled in with so much dark by sunset that it nearly matches the thick patch on his chin, which he prefers. Despite the cover, I know Dan is clean. I can connect with Dan. His dark hair doesn't hide dark secrets. When I study him, the beard doesn't change what I see: sincerity.

It's one of the reasons he's my original go-to for wild science story ideas—like tackling deer. Together, we've counted cutthroat trout, backpacked fish to high mountain lakes, and taken our little kids on big river trips. He's a fisheries biologist, but on deer-collaring day, he shows up.

"Catch-and-release deer hunting," he says while we're sardined under sagebrush. "What's not to love?"

The Idaho Department of Fish and Game sets hunting seasons based on animal counts. To count wild animals, you have to put an electronic collar on some of them. That collar sends a tracking signal so herds are easier to find for counting throughout the year. The department collars deer by herding them into yards and yards of netting stretched across a valley void to create a funnel in the winter. The chopper pushes deer down the hill cattle-drive style. The deer are in flight mode when they hit the net, and then they fight. They're trapped, but not tranquilized. They're untangled from the net, then held down by humans instead. This is all done with a few feet of snow on the ground to soften the blows for both beast and biologist.

A tube of soft fabric cut from the stretchy sleeve of an extra-large T-shirt is pulled over the deer's muzzle, covering its eyes. Its snout and mouth are exposed so it can breathe, but it can't see. I don't know about you, but I panic more when I can't see. I must make sure my shots are level with the horizon, and I need to see to do that. Fortunately, once an animal is netted, I can lift my eyes for a solid frame adjustment, but the animal can't. Somewhere along the way, scientists figured out that covering an animal's eyes so they can't see the humans holding them down actually calms them.

They're hugged tight for ten minutes while measurements are taken and GPS collars are given. The deer kick, squirm, and groan, but bound off unharmed and sporting a new necklace as the "ship" sends another batch into the biologists.

Round one is done and I hear Curtis over the radio, asking, "Is Millgate still with us?"

He's not doubting my skills. He's doubting the less than ideal conditions. He's dealt with his share of reporters regretting their decision to come along. That can show in a story, or lack of a story in some cases. The last thing I want to do on any assignment is bail. That's bad form during the situation and even worse for future work.

I once shared a shoot with a videographer who was unprepared for difficult conditions. We were on snowshoes in a canyon that was literally frozen solid. It was minus twenty degrees. I carried my camera batteries in my armpits to keep them from freezing. Ice crystals grew inside my nostrils and my lungs felt frosted, but I wasn't the one to go when the going got tough—he was.

There's a difference between dangerous and difficult, and I'm always gauging the two. The time I parked my news car behind a state trooper's car instead of in front of it at a snowstorm pileup cost me a sideswipe by another car that would have killed me had I stepped out to shoot video. Always let the law's lights, not your logo, be the first thing approaching traffic encounters in a hazardous situation, especially on black ice. That dumb move by me was dangerous, stupid, and, to my embarrassment, snarled traffic, making the interstate even more dangerous. I moved my car, shot footage from the shoulder with quaking hands, and cried all the way back to the station. That was obscenely dangerous.

The cold day in the canyon wasn't dangerous, just difficult. I ended up with beautifully breathtaking frozen footage that I'll never be able to replicate. The other videographer ended up waiting for us at the truck because the conditions proved too difficult for him. He knew his limits and respected them, but as a woman I don't want to come across as limited, so I extend myself by preparing for the difficult.

I earn my place among the men I work with because I learned early on that whiners don't get invited again. Say you're cold and hungry, or it's too hard, and you're out. I wear plenty of layers, pack plenty of food, and when it's too hard, I push even harder, because I want to be included more than I want to be comforted. I endured twenty years of being excluded from Scout camp; I'm not interested in sitting out another twenty.

I whined once, and only once, when hiking with my dad. He told me to turn back early. I did, and later he told me about the grand view I missed at the trail's end. I don't turn back early anymore. No matter how unbearable or difficult fieldwork is at times, it has to be done—it helps biologists understand what's happening beyond city limits. If animal populations decline, researchers will know about it even if they can't determine the cause of the decline right away.

Gathering data isn't a desk job until an animal is wearing a trackable collar. The desk job aspect has never been for me, because it equates to visually poor story material. Give me the collaring part over a desk any day. I make sure the deer-capture crew—and every other crew, for that matter—knows two things about me: I carry my own weight and I do my job well. So yeah, Curtis, Millgate is still with you. Gender is irrelevant when it's deer doing the damage. They kick teeth and bruise bellies without discretion.

When there's a lull in the capture action, I abandon my sagebrush shield and stand. My knees are battered from crouching and crawling. As the ship flies off to find another herd, I wander off to do what everyone does every few hours. As a lady, I need more cover, so I have to walk farther than the men for this chore, but I don't mind. The walk works out the kinks.

This solo squat routine is one I've done many times over the years. Other than sleeping alone in the dark, going to the bathroom is about the only other alone thing I do when I'm working with beards. I see the same thing every time I go. The snow closer to the work site is pocked with yellow and brown patches. One is urine. The other is spit tainted with chewing tobacco. I keep walking until the patches disappear, then walk farther just to be sure I'm out of sight. There's no need for fanfare; I take care of business and get back to work just like everyone else does.

"Is there anyone in camp, besides me, who doesn't chew?" I joke upon my return.

We have thirty-five deer collared by day's end. It's success for the crew, but heartache for me. I have only one of two cameras; the other is missing. I attached it to Curtis, but it didn't stick. He lost it. We're somewhere north of Mud Lake, Idaho, in ankle-deep snow, and we're leaving. The lost camera, and all its footage, is staying. It's not coming home with me like the dunker camera on the Green River did.

"I hope you have insurance," Curtis says as we tear down nets.

"Take a look at what I do for a living. I run around in the woods with you," I say, gathering the net as it spools in the snow. "I might be crazy, but not crazy enough to work uninsured."

The lost camera was buried in snow for three months. Curtis found it while counting sage grouse during the spring thaw. It still works.

COURTING BULL ELK

"IT WOULD BE so great if you would just go ahead and fart."

"Fart?"

"Yeah. Loosen up the awkwardness of having a woman with us. Make us feel more comfortable."

We're hiking single file, in whispers, on a single track. The request comes from the front man. What he means is, make me fit when I don't. I sense an insecure beard ahead. The beard behind laughs.

"I don't fart on cue," I say into the predawn dark between Front Beard's back and my face. "But I will talk like a trucker if you make me miss this shot."

The face at my back barks. It's a barely leashed snicker in the silence.

"It's too dark for a shot," Front Beard says.

"I have a feeling you're still going to be talking when the sun rises," I say. "And there will be plenty of light for a shot by then."

"I'll stop talking if you fart." Front Beard again.

Now Back Beard speaks.

"I'm going to lose it if you fart, and the elk will hear me lose it. I'm a loud laugher. Please don't fart."

Good. Back Beard doesn't need me to fart. Back Beard doesn't care if I fit, and I don't care either. Let Front Beard fester as I, the female, stay sandwiched between two beards. I find Front Beard's insecurity exhausting, but it isn't devastating. I'm here, aren't I? I'm done being devastated. Done a long time ago.

When I'm in the woods with men, I'm forever the elephant in the room. In this case, a farting elephant, if Mark Casias had his way. He's Front Beard, also known as the elk whisperer. He can be known as whatever he wants as long as he puts me on elk.

I'm in New Mexico's Carson National Forest, near Taos, to see newly restored elk habitat, but frankly, there's nothing new about New Mexico, from the aging red peppers strung across every porch that I pass to the crumbling crucifixes perched in a prominent position at every Catholic church erected on every corner. Even the locals, with their weathered and wrinkled skin browned by heat and heredity, carry years of wisdom on their faces.

The time-gone-awry illusion is alluring. I like the look of New Mexico through my lens, but the countless dirty looks locals give me put me back on high alert. I'm the gringa ordering "Christmas" (green and red chile) on my burrito with no trace of linguistic variation in my dime-a-dozen white girl voice, the voice I learned to project while wet with whiskey courage. It's clear I'm an unwelcome outsider, and although I can't blame them, I don't have much of a choice if I want to chase this story.

Back Beard is Garrett VeneKlasen, GVK as I call him. He's the enthusiastic hunter–conservationist who came up with this story idea. He put Mark and me together, which in the end proves wise, but during the meet, greet, and fart part, I'm doubtful.

Creepy comments aside, Mark and Garrett are the tormented heroes in this story. They're two of the thousands of off-highway vehicle (OHV) riders who ripped up the forest. They're also the two who willingly pulled their rigs out of the woods so the wildlife could return.

We stop in Garrett's "church" for interviews. His church is my kind of church. Well-aged aspen trunks drawing the eye so high, my long hair falls away from my face when I look up. The branches release blessings of yellow leaves, their falling shimmer an offering of gold coins. It's a holy place where unholy things once happened.

"I did ride in a lot of areas and I regret riding where we rode," Mark says while I clip a mic to the front of his shirt. "There was just so much damage to the forest, and I'm guilty of that."

I record Garrett's interview after Mark's. Garrett expresses just as much guilt, but his confession is laced with repentance.

"There's some regret, but there's also some pride in what we've accomplished locally," Garrett says. "We're the ones who wrecked it and we've been instrumental in trying to fix it."

The fix is called a sanctuary, areas you can drive around but not through. There are two in the Carson. The small chunks of refuge worked, and elk returned within two years. I want to see these sanctuaries. These men know where they are.

Mark may outright ask me to break wind, but Garrett is just as devious in his own way. He's as unpretentious as I am and we goof around like siblings when the moment warrants. But when it's time to work, his intensity matches mine.

"Anyone who has the physical and mental ability to follow us over hill and over dell for days on end without even complaining while bogged down with equipment is incredible," Garrett had said when he'd convinced Mark I was the right woman for this job—even if I don't fit the gender mold Mark prefers to hunt with.

Garrett's endorsement worked, and into the woods we went, with Mark asking for natural bodily functions while the natural world reveals itself over a handful of quiet days between archery and rifle season.

The pressure during that window moves from the elk to me. Shouldering the responsibility of collecting award-winning elk footage is a tremendous burden, because shooting the wild with a camera is harder than shooting it with a weapon, especially for me. I shoot still photos with my left eye and video footage with my right eye. Each medium has its own camera. To master either of them effectively, I don't need three seconds to take aim; I need thirty, and I may need another dozen thirty seconds to really make the most of what's going on.

To ease my serious face, as Garrett calls it, he wears a decaying set of fake teeth that make him look hilarious. He says they're his summer teeth: as in, *some are* there, *some are* not. He slips them into his beard-bordered mouth when I'm most stressed, and flashes a huge crooked grin every time my eyes find him through the trees. Camo hides him well, but I never miss the teeth. It lightens my mood despite the heavy frustration and serious fear running through my vibrating veins.

The pressure to perform nearly buckles me when the first elk approaches the grove we're squatting in. It's a male, a bull elk, and he's advancing because Mark is mimicking the call of another bull—he's bugling. Bulls don't like other bulls in their mating territory so he's here to push us out . . . if he can find us. He's charging and I'm recording because it's a beauty of a bull with a heavy rack, wide body, and long legs. I'm crouched on my knees, trying not to bump my tripod and blow the shot. It's a compromising position during an amazing moment, but I must hold still so the bull doesn't spook.

"You can hear his breathing. It's an adrenaline rush big-time," Mark quietly tells me between bugles. "You work so hard. Sometimes some of these calling episodes are well over an hour."

The elk sniffs the air, scrapes the ground with his hooves, and keeps advancing. He's ten feet from my lens, trying to figure out two things: Where the hell is the bull that's bugling a challenge, and what the hell is crouched on the ground right in front of me?

That's when I realize this whole deal is a bad idea. It's the rut. The bull is looking for a date. I definitely don't want to be his date. He's close—too close. I have to zoom out to fit him in frame. In the stillness, the bull hears the lens gears engage, raises his rack, then runs away. I have my first of many amazing elk shots for the day and I'm shaking like California in quake mode.

"That interactive moment with a creature is what burns in your mind," Garrett says as we stand from the joint-cracking position of a crouch held for too many minutes. "That bull is the essence of the wild world boiled down into one perfect creature."

Perfection has me disoriented. I need a few minutes to collect myself. I stand and move toward an open meadow to warm my dew-soaked jacket. Mind you, I took a tongue-lashing on day one for wearing a jacket tumbled dry with sweet-smelling fabric softener. Mark claimed the elk could smell me from miles away the first two days and that's why we got skunked. That screwup was on me and I was embarrassed. It's now day three. I'm plenty dirty, my jacket stinks, and we are seeing elk everywhere. Maybe the elk whisperer knows what he's talking about.

With our first wild talking episode wrapped up, we meet in the clearing and joke about the shot being so good that we need a post-relations cigarette, but since none of us smoke, we celebrate by strategizing our next stalk.

I knelt in standby mode for hours on the last bull. That zaps camera juice and I need to reload. The ever-grinning Garrett begged to help carry some of my equipment, so I gave him my extra batteries. I rarely let others pack my gear. If something goes wrong, I want it on me, not on them. Garrett is the reason why.

He starts rifling through his pack, awkwardly laughs, dumps the pack contents in the dirt, and then spits his fake teeth out to confess he doesn't have the batteries. I want to kick in his real teeth. We are three hours from the truck. We are in the thick of bulls trying to get lucky, and I have half a battery left. My bowels may do much more than fart at this point.

This screwup is on Garrett. I'm embarrassed for him and I'm mad at him, burning mad. But in the toxic stew I'm brewing, I suddenly boil with clarity. We all screw up out here. Not just women who supposedly don't belong out here, but men, too. Everyone fumbles in the forest. How you recover is what sets you apart, not your gender. Recovery requires creativity and optimism and that has nothing to do with chest hair. Quit in a critical moment like this and you won't come back, so just figure out a fix and get on with it.

Realizing blunders don't discriminate gives me a severe head spin. I like the fairness of that concept, but the actual awareness of it throws me off balance. I have to bend over. I breathe deep five times, hands propped on my knees. I give myself one more minute to recover creatively, then I straighten with an optimistic plan. My video camera will stay off until the last possible second, and then I'll roll through the heat of things for as long as the equipment and the elk allow.

It's dicey, but I do it. As Mark calls them in, I collect footage. Garrett stays behind us. One bugler comes so close while he's sending out song, I feel his breath raise the hair on my forearms. His head is low, rack swinging back and forth like a grain thresher, and his blond-coated belly billows in and out with bursts of sound when he raises his neck to the sky to scream. He's beyond impressive. I guarantee that bull scores raunchy dates with cows.

"He's studly-hung-well and he knows it," Garrett whispers, leaning toward us, hoping I've moved on from the screwup, which I have. "A bull like that doesn't even need to date, and foreplay is optional."

Collecting my story isn't optional. That's why I won't leave empty-handed just because crude comments come with screwups in wild territory. I don't encourage vulgarity, but I don't run when it's delivered, either. Sometimes I think the words spoken with spite are specifically designed to make me run. But I won't: that would be giving in and giving up. I don't give in and I don't give up on a story worth telling. Elk on the return is worth talking about no matter how much BS blows between bugles. That's the reality of the male-dominated profession in which I earn my keep.

And this story is full of potential. I have a week's worth of elk money shots collected in one morning on the last day of the video shoot with only one battery between us. Ridiculous? Yes. Impossible? No. Now, that's something to really grin about.

Garrett and I still swap scary teeth photos. Mark is still waiting for me to fart.

COUNTING SHEEP

NOW I'M NOT chasing elk, but rather dodging a crowd. Easier said than done with only one working leg. Doc says I can attend outdoor shows, but I can't walk them. I'm learning to live with a rod in my leg, so walking is a ways down the road, but I'm at a show so that's a start.

One of the best things about attending outdoor shows is running into people I've done stories with, like the people you're meeting in these chapters. They gather from all over the country and I'm with them in a scooter. You know, the electric kind plugged in for recharge along the wall near the main entrance of shopping malls and grocery stores and convention centers. I rented one and I'm riding it. I'm a fast walker and it's a slow roller. It's frustrating and it's weird. I think I look weak, and I don't like the vulnerability of that.

Everyone is used to seeing me upright on two strong sticks (my legs) with another set of sticks (my tripod) over my shoulder, chasing something wild and worthy of lens attention. I'm doing none of that. I'm riding a scooter in Sunday stroll mode.

My recently repaired limb bends at the knee now and it's tucked close to the scooter's basket and handlebars. It's covered with loose, stretchy pants so its disjointed and discolored condition doesn't sick anyone out.

My fat foot doesn't fit in a shoe yet, so it's sporting a light-blue hospital sock, the kind with white grippy dots on the bottom for anti-slip traction. As if I could put my foot down anyway. I can't; it's too early, and my bones would buckle. Again.

My neck is stiff from looking up at everyone because they're standing and I'm sitting on a scooter. I really don't like the scooter, but it's necessary.

The show is miles of booths and millions of stairs. I avoid stairs by finding elevators. I'm in one of those elevators when a skinny man about my size in weight, but much taller, slips in right before the doors slide closed. He has a red beard and bloodshot eyes, shifty eyes. I decide I don't like him as soon as he pushes me out of my scooter. Pushes me!

I hit the dirty elevator carpet on elbow and hip, my broken leg wedged under the seat. The elevator doors open, Red Beard rips my scooter away, ripping my new repairs to rubble, and taking my ride—and my backpack that's in the basket—with him. I can't crawl out fast enough to beat the closing doors let alone chase the stealer. The doors close. I open my eyes.

I'm crying. It's just another dream. Drug-induced dreams are crazy, so real, but crazy. And stealing dreams might suck more than falling dreams. Falling dreams hurt physically; stealing dreams hurt emotionally.

I'm not at a show. I'm still at home, recovering, in my bed instead of on the couch because it's the middle of the night. I transfer my body up the stairs to bed at night.

My husband slides over with reassurance. I ask him if he's so far away from me in our bed because I'm ugly. He laughs himself awake and says he can't tell if I'm ugly in the dark, but that's not why he sleeps hanging off the other side of the bed.

He's scared he'll hurt my injuries in his sleep, so he's staying far away. I started reducing my pain medication this week. I want my memory retention back, but reducing pills means I sleep in fits because I can feel my body trying to repair itself. He doesn't want to undo any repairs or add any agony, so he's giving me space. I tell him I'm up because someone stole my scooter.

"You don't have a scooter," he whispers in the dark. "And if you did, why would someone steal it?"

"So I can't chase them when they steal all of my other stuff," I whisper back. "My cameras, my money, my phone. With so many stairs and no leg to climb them with, I'd have to resort to sitting on the sidewalk hoping you'd know where to look for me."

"I know when and where to look for you," he says with a yawn. "Now go back to sleep."

I'm done sleeping, but he's not. He slides way over to the right again and starts breathing deeply. I shove my sagging right foot into a pillow. The process of lightly pressing against a pillow is supposed to stretch my wilting arch and folding toes, both withering due to lack of use. I wiggle my toes, feel my foot tingle, then start counting sheep.

Bighorn sheep. They're cool. Rams, lambs, and ewes. They're all cool with their coats of one color, invisibility. It's nearly impossible to find bighorn sheep for two reasons. First, their fur matches the landscape they live among. It matches *exactly*. Snow is their only disadvantage, because they don't turn white in winter like weasels do. Second, there aren't a lot of invisible coats left in the West. In many places, bighorns don't exist anymore. In other places, herds hover under a dozen.

I'm covering a story about one of those on-the-verge-of-blinking-out herds in early spring. The eastern Idaho desert is mostly bare of snow, but no matter, we find the herd. One ewe was collared last year. The redundant radio beep of her movements tells us where she is and where the other animals wandering with her are, including a few young rams. Biologists want to collar one of the young rams then watch where it wanders, hoping it knows where more bighorn baby makers hang out.

On these kinds of stories—any wildlife story, really—I don't dictate how scenes unfold or in what order I shoot my shots. Usually I get footage before the interview so I can relate my questions to what I see, but that's about the most I can ask for when I have no control over what happens.

There's no script or shot sheet like in the movies. I can't tell the animals to stand in the best light, and I certainly don't tell the people to say things that put them, or the issue, in the best light.

During shoots, my microphones are in use even when I'm not doing interviews. I like to clip wireless mics to people while they're in action so I can pick up their personality and story intel in addition to an official interview. People clearly know they're mic'd because I ask them to wear the mic. I also have

to invade their space to run wires through their clothes while testing audio transmission into my earpiece. Once that's done, they wander off to do their thing and I wander off to do mine, all the while listening.

They talk about what they're doing, and I match my shots to their action. The play-by-play works even in wide shots. I'm out of reasonable hearing range, but I hear everything because the bud in my ear lets me eavesdrop. The problem with openly putting a mic on someone for natural sound is a few minutes after you clip on the mic they know about, they forget they're wearing it. More importantly, they forget I can hear everything they say, even when I'm far away.

It's unintentional and it's inevitable. I've run many a river-bank on early mornings, ripping earbuds out of my head as the guy wearing the other end of the audio feed wades into the willows to relieve himself of too much breakfast brew. Now that, I don't want to hear, but it's harmless; it's not what hurts me.

Some of what's said does hurt me, or it could if I let it, and it usually happens when I walk away from the scene for a wide shot. I'm still looking with my lens and listening with my wires, but I'm walking away, out of normal human hearing range.

"You see her rack?"

"She married?"

"Happily married?"

I roll my eyes and continue working like their banter is beyond my range. And truthfully, for that matter, it's beyond my bother.

But in the huddle over the bighorn getting a GPS collar attached to its neck, I hear this as I walk away for a wide shot.

"Where is she going? Does she even know what she's doing? Nothing is over there. Is she any good at what she does?"

A wireless mic picks up the voice of the body it's on, but it also picks up voices attached to bodies huddled close to one another, not clear enough to be used in a story, but clear enough for me to hear in my earpiece.

"Is she any good?"

Seriously? He's seriously asking that? And right now? Seriously? His blatant disregard for my work ethic just because I'm a "she" infuriates me. I didn't assume he's an ass just because he's a guy, but I want to now. I want to turn around and yell, "I can hear you, asshat!" But I keep marching away, not turning back. He doesn't know I can hear him and I don't want him to know he makes me feel vulnerable. I silently shake my head while walking toward the spot I've already spied for a wide shot. He's trying to discount my personal integrity, but I'm not about to let him screw with my professional intentions.

I don't know everyone in the huddle, but I bet my skills that it's the guy with the handlebar mustache spilling the "any good" question into the dusty air. Yes, a handlebar mustache—it's still fashionable in the West. Sometimes it's authentic, but other times it's just trendy. This guy is too old for trendy, so he must be wearing the mustache unironically.

We're working in dusty air, so add that to everyone's disheveled appearance. We're coated in powdery soil, but it disguises nothing. Shallow insults don't hide easily. We're in the desert and most of the snow was sucked out of the ground months ago. Summer rains are yet to come. Dry earth grinds between my teeth like the "any good" guy, grinding on my last nerve.

We're in a dust bowl, with all the loose particles raised by a chopper chasing sheep from the snowline of the high country down into the flat lowlands of the desert below. There are a dozen bighorn sheep running for their lives, and one takes the fall for them all. Well, the fall and the collar. He's not dead, just held down, collared and then released.

I want to see the huddle rise when the ram is released. That's why I move away from the action for a wide shot. The best action is coming soon, and it will be best from farther away: the run-away scene. I know exactly what I'm doing, but that one guy doesn't.

"Is she any good?" he asks again, the rest of the huddle concentrating on their quest more than his query.

I stop walking, spread my tripod's legs in the dirt between sagebrush and bitter brush, and click my camera in place, all eyes on my equipment like I don't hear a thing, but I hear everything. Including the reply.

"You'll know the answer to that when you see her story," says an unidentified voice I'd like to meet. "Now, on the count of three, we're letting this guy go. One, two, three."

I'm rolling, huddle rising, dust lifting. All humans. No animal in sight. More rolling, rising, lifting. The ram springs then sinks. He doesn't spring higher than the hands in the huddle that held him down. He springs again. The huddle backs off. Again with more effort, more space. Spring! The ram flops on its face. Its front legs don't work. Something went wrong during capture. This ram won't release. It wants to, but can't. Now the huddle of humans is so far from the ram, it's out of my wide shot and in my personal space. We're all watching, hoping the animal rebounds and runs. Its front legs just fell asleep, that's all.

That's not the case, not the case at all. Bighorn sheep are capture sensitive. Just like pronghorn antelope will panic themselves into a heart attack during capture if you're not careful, bighorn don't handle holdings well either.

I don't control the wild. The wild controls my stories, and in this case the story is bad. In a herd of shrinking bighorns, one of the few remaining rams is leaving the herd for good. It dies the next day. Collar mission failed, wildlife wasted.

It's not pretty. It's not common, but it happens and it happens while I'm watching. It has to go in the story, and I have a duty to explain why capture is risky and why this type of work is still worth the risk. Personally, I don't like how this particular story ends, but professionally I'm proud of its accuracy, its truth, and its reality. It's a solid story, proof that even though my storytelling skills are strong, the main character, the ram, still died.

Makes me wonder, is he—that guy with the handlebar mustache—any good?

OWLS IN THE OUTHOUSE

REMEMBERING THE RAM that can't run makes me anxious about my leg, so I get out of bed, find my crutches in the dark, and hobble past my husband, who is hanging off the mattress, snoring slightly. I move toward our master bath, not silently. That's impossible in my current condition. I mean really, all my years of ballet and I'm about as graceful on crutches as a hippo in a tree swing.

I bang into the rails at the foot of our bed, rattling everything that's in contact with the bed frame, including my husband. I swear and swerve away from that hazard and hit the dresser. Next, a chair. I quickly assess appendages, then keep going. I haven't done any more damage to my body, just my bedroom. I got this. The bathroom door is barely beyond the chair I just stubbed.

I once broke my pinkie toe on a LEGO while stumbling around in the dark among toys scattered on the floor by my kids. If I step on another LEGO right now with my one functioning foot, I guarantee the whole house is going to wake up alarmed with me, the ungraceful hippo, swinging in the center ring of the circus.

Knob within reach, I close the bathroom door behind me resourcefully so I don't disturb anyone when I turn the light on. I could go downstairs and really get out of my husband's hair, but it's too early to go down. I don't want to start my stay on the couch yet.

I only use the stairs in each direction once a day. Down them to the couch in the morning and up them at night to go to bed. The sun isn't up yet, so it's not morning. I stay upstairs to bathe before going down.

Our master bath is deep, water-to-your-neck deep if you want. That's what I want, but I don't get it. I'm allowed three inches of water, about the depth of a festering cesspool growing red bacteria in a low spot of lava rock. Three inches of the hottest water I can stand and that's how I soak without my leg soaking. It's propped up on a foldable black plastic stool my husband added for me as my leg's resting spot above the water. Keeps the stitches, holes, and scabs from getting wet.

I firmly lower myself into my bath, my arms starting to muscle more from crutching. That's a useful discovery. Then I make sure my right leg is high and dry on the stool my boys first used post-potty training. That's right: the pee stool from their toilet is now in my tub. When they first learned to pee like men, they weren't tall like men. Their bellies, instead of their knees, were at the bowl. I bought a folding stool for them to stand on, giving them proper height for better aim. When the boys grew, the pee stool moved to the closet. It recently found new purpose in my tub.

I wonder what my bone doctor thinks of that: keeping bones dry, but using a stool once saturated in urine to do it. Deep down, disgusting. That's what it is, but hold on. It's brilliant in its utility. At least, that's what I decide. The decision is a huge development for me. I'm not into people germs, but I want a bath so badly that I'm willing to put the pee stool in my tub to get it.

I close my eyes, thinking the setup is super. My ears amplify sound when my eyes are shut, so I start listening, rather than looking, for action. Not much moving in the house. The boys are asleep still, the deep purple of early rise not enough to poke at them yet. I hear the ice maker clank in the kitchen one level lower than where I am. It's turning over another batch of cubes in its internal bucket. I'll make good use of that batch in my ice packs in a few hours. Other than that, the house is still. But outside, there's activity.

I keep my eyes closed and listen harder, holding still to be sure.

"Who, who, who are you?"

Yep, an owl. It's north of the house, beyond the neighborhood, in what's left of an undeveloped field I used to run in and had cut a cross-country ski trail through the day before my leg broke. Bet that's buried by now. Stop sulking. Concentrate.

Hooting owl here. Your leg is no big deal in the big picture. An owl is. Urban sprawl is pushing them farther out, but this one is coming in.

It's probably hunting. For a meal or a mate, I can't be sure. I don't know what the call does in the dark, but I recognize it every time I hear it and I hear it more in the winter.

"Who, who, who are you?"

The call teases me to answer. It's closer to the house now and a bit to the east, toward the bald eagle nest near our neighborhood. The eagles aren't there much in the winter, but I bet their food supply still is.

I listen to the owl until its call drops like an unanswered ring going to voicemail or, even more abrupt, disconnecting. I picture the owl wrapping up its hunt, silencing sound, and hooding its lids over its bright yellow-orbed eyes like hanging up a phone.

Owls are funny creatures. Me thinking about them while I'm in the bathroom is funnier. Especially as I recall the last time I fancied owls in an outhouse.

I was shooting scenic footage in an unknown and rarely visited place in southern Idaho called Curlew National Grassland, the only grassland in the Intermountain West that's managed by the U.S. Forest Service. Even more unknown than this arid place is its potty problem. That's the reason why there's a man on the roof of one of those classic bowel-brown outhouses.

Above the short sea of sage and sedge, I see him shuffling around near a black pipe. That pipe vents the unmentionable fumes festering inside the small building no one wants to enter, but eventually everyone has to.

I unhinge my camera from the tripod and make a run for the restroom. Chris Colt, Caribou-Targhee National Forest wildlife biologist, is at the base of the ladder leading up to the man holding a drill on the toilet's roof. The exchange goes something like this:

"What are you doing?"

"Putting a screen on the vent to keep birds out," Chris says.

"Wait. What? Birds in the bathroom?" I say, stunned.

"In the worst part of the bathroom and more often than you think."

I'm grossed out and interested at the same time. I dig for facts while staring at a situation so foul that I should look away, but I can't help myself. Owls burrow in bathroom vents and end up trapped in outhouse toilets, unintentionally covered in human feces. There's a story here and I'll fight a phobia to get it.

I'm a germ freak. I don't mind outdoor dirt; it's people germs that freak me out, and outhouses are full of people germs, among other things. I'll hold my serious business rather than hover over an outhouse hole. And if the situation is dire, I must inspect the hole before I hover.

I once confessed my outhouse inspection ritual around a campfire and I've never heard the end of it. Apparently I'm the only one who looks in the hole? Hold up. Let's be honest here. Apparently I'm the only one who *admits* they look in the hole. That's what it really is. Regardless, my campfire confession has me eternally stuck on groover duty during river trips.

The groover is the portable toilet you haul along on multi-day river trips in the wilderness where you must pack out, like Idaho's Middle Fork of the Salmon River. It's called the groover because way back in the day, it was an old ammo can that put grooves in your backside when you sat on it. It's bigger today, and boxier, but it's still a stench fest.

My so-far-from-afraid-of-germs-that-I-don't-like-it-when-he-touches-my-food friend Rob Thornberry loves to hassle me about my anti-germ stance. On multiday river trips I watch his face morph from shaved to shaggy, never changing his place in my studies of him. He's intense, crabby, and easy to argue with, whether haired or hairless.

In his eyes, there's nothing more spectacular than me on a raft with the groover riding shotgun. In my eyes, it's horrid. Especially when the metal box with sharp corners pops the raft, and my husband and I spend all day listening to air hiss out while hoping we don't swamp our kids in white water before we can patch the leak.

Germ freak or not, groover duty really is the worst part of all the best trips. But I'm stuck with it now, and retracting my inspection ritual isn't going to get me out of it. So I own my quirks and keep looking down the hole before I hover.

My reasons for looking are warranted. The boys on Curlew bathroom duty are verifying that, so I move in rather than run away. I look down the hole because something, other than the obvious, is down there. Something that shouldn't be down there.

"That large-diameter pipe is pretty enticing to certain species of wildlife like cavity-nesting owls," Chris says while holding the ladder steady outside the outhouse door. "They see it as a tree cavity, like a tree with the top broken off that's rotted inside. They climb down in there and maybe make a nest and then they can't get out."

I don't want to go in, but Joe Foust will. He's the Boise National Forest wildlife biologist who rescued a boreal owl from a bathroom in 2010.

"When I got there, there was a Post-it note on door: 'Owl in toilet. Don't use. Go down the road for other toilet.' I looked down there and sure enough, he was just sitting there looking up at me," Joe says. "It got a little messy when I tried to get him in the net. He didn't fair well after that. Nor did I. He went ballistic and started bouncing up and down and just got soaked."

So did Joe, who took a few unpleasant pictures of the retrieval operation deep in the bowels of the Boise National Forest campground bathroom. Those pictures ended up at the Teton Raptor Center in Wilson, Wyoming, where David Watson works.

"It's not a sexy thing to study, but it happens all over the country with all kinds of cavity-nesting birds," David says. "They're looking for that quiet, dark space. They don't realize that pipe sticking up out of the toilet is a death trap for them."

David is proudly known as the "Poo-Poo King." He's the director for the center's Poo-Poo Project (that's short for Port-o-Potty Owl Project). He's also one of the creative minds behind the twelve-inch Poo-Poo screen keeping birds out of sewage. The one-piece steel screen, selling for $29.95, comes with four screws and installs in five minutes. Government agencies and nonprofit organizations in all fifty states are installing them. Most of the vented vault toilets are on public land in remote places where the commute costs more than the construction project.

"The biggest difficulty is the time it takes to drive to your next toilet," Chris says. "You get there, there's maybe two toilets on a site, it takes ten to fifteen minutes and you're done and moving on."

The Teton Raptor Center sold its ten thousandth Poo-Poo screen in 2017 to, ironically, a concrete company in Montana that makes vault toilets. While ten thousand sounds like market saturation, that's really just a drop in the bucket when you consider the overwhelming number of outhouses nationwide.

"I hate to see some owl go down there, get stuck, and get killed, or worse, still be alive and have to be fished out," Chris says while folding the ladder in preparation for the drive to the next pit stop. "People can argue that it's crazy, but if you can stop one owl from going down there, it was probably worth it."

My vote: totally worth it. Chris is screening every outhouse, twenty-five, in the Caribou-Targhee National Forest Westside Ranger District. I'll be more than willing to verify that by looking up at the pipe instead of down into the hole the next time I visit Curlew.

THE SAGE GROUSE STRUT

I DRAIN THE tub an inch and add another inch of fresher, hotter water, keeping the stool top, and my scabs, above the liquid line. The sun isn't up yet and neither is my husband. I'll soak a little longer in here, losing more hours of sleep.

I'm well aware of the many disasters delivered due to lack of sleep. I'm also aware of the rare potential that develops when puttering around in the darkness. Such potential pulls me from my bed long before the rest of the world opens its sleep-crusted eyes. It's the possibility of witnessing the wild at its finest. It's the promise of seeing the dance in the desert before it disappears. That's why I get up for grouse.

I've watched sage grouse strut for years. Since long before the bird became the vanishing symbol of the West. I even woke up early to watch sage grouse the year I was pregnant with my first son. I crawled around in the sagebrush with wildlife biologist Daryl Meints. We spied on grouse doing their spring thing and quietly captured it all on camera during the first hour of daylight. Then I looked at my pants. The silent stalk instantly ended when I saw bird poop smeared across my knees. Daryl laughed. I puked. Daryl laughed harder.

"Wow, Millgate," he'd said while handing me a wad of tissue from his glove box. "I didn't know you were such a girl."

And I didn't know a bachelor would be the first person I'd confess my pending motherhood to, but that's how it turned out. I explained my sudden squeamish side as morning sickness, and Daryl knew I was having a baby before my own mother did.

I think of that morning with Daryl every time I go looking for sage grouse. Puking in sagebrush was a one-time deal. Watching sage grouse is an annual affair.

I particularly like heading two hours north to document one of the largest leks in Idaho. Leks are open strips of land chosen by male sage grouse. They choose areas void of cover because they want to strut for females without anything getting in the way of their display. It's the wild's version of a strip tease in a spotlight. I head to my favorite lek in April, mating season, when the tease factor is high.

I load my backpack and tripod into my truck, pull out of the garage, check the milk bin on my porch, then head north. I like checking the milk bin on my porch. Correction. I like looking at the milk bin on my porch. I look at it more than I look in it. There's only milk in it every other Thursday, but I look at it every time I leave the house. Even when I leave the house at o'dark thirty, pre-sunrise, for sage grouse.

Sometimes I smile when I look at my milk bin. Other times I frown, but only when I'm alone. If my kids, my husband, or anyone else is with me, I lift the frown into a smile. I prefer smiling. It feels stronger than a weak frown, especially when I'm looking at my milk bin.

My milk bin is my pride displayed on our porch. It's my version of fitting in shown off for the world to see. It's metal, not cardboard like the charity box left on our porch when I was little. It's sturdy, not soggy. It has a solid lift-top lid, not four flimsy flaps. The milk jugs placed inside it every other Thursday by Milkman Mike are clear and recyclable, not crusty cartons dumped when drained. And the color of the cow on the container . . . my favorite part: a bold, blazing red.

I signed up for dairy home delivery shortly after my husband and I bought our house. I put the new silver-shiny bin on my front porch, stepped away to admire it from my front lawn, and said, "It's a major award!" Like the dad winning the legendary leg lamp in the movie *A Christmas Story.*

To me, it *is* a major award. I clean it every time I Windex my front windows, which is weekly. I don't care who sees it or who drinks what's inside it. There's success in that bin, not shame. I can afford milk! That bin and the local dairy products I buy to go inside it biweekly are my own "I fit" statement. No one else values my version of fit like I do, and they don't have to. That's why it's mine. That's why I smile. Except on the days that I frown.

On frown days, failure and fear are riding hard on my native surface. It happens when I'm finding typos in my already published story. When I'm losing opportunities because of another so-called shortcoming in my skill set. When some "any good" guy tries forever more to make me feel like I'm less. Or is it me always making me feel like I'm less? It's possible women make themselves feel inferior without any help from society and sometimes because of society. Either way, shame can be self-inflicted. I know mine can be. No input from "any good" guy needed on my hardest days. How messed up is that? I see myself as undeserving of long-term success when I don't measure up to my own expectations in the short-term. To pursue the unexpected while also discovering the pushback caused by that pursuit is sometimes internal, not external; that in and of itself is unexpected.

In my mind, I'm never very far from where I've been. I'm never being good enough, trying hard enough, working well enough, or moving fast enough. That's how I tick and there's no undoing that. That mental struggle causes me physical angst. My voice cuts, coughs, chokes. I push *never* down with a gag and a gulp of air, but it doesn't disappear. Neither will that bin. It's my major award. My look-how-far-I've-come confirmation when failure and fear try forcing their way in. The bin is never going away. It's part of my strut.

BIRDS IN A BAR

DURING THE TWO-HOUR drive from my front porch, where the milk bin is perched, to the ranch gate where sage grouse strut, the sky shifts from sleep to sun and I shift my thoughts from bins to birds.

The Nature Conservancy owns the undeveloped ranch near Dubois, where one of the largest sage grouse leks in Idaho still puts on a solid show. Ron Laird manages the ranch and monitors the lek.

I wouldn't say he's a rancher, but rather, he *is* ranch. Unshaven stubble fences his jawline like the barbed-wire boundary he exists within. From his faded, dusty denim to the peppered pattern of his hair, he's sturdy and rugged and, like I said, ranch.

Wrangling cattle seems more his nature, but regardless of roundups, Ron starts every spring day contently tucked inside a camo-colored tent, watching birds dance in front of a long lens that he points through one of the blind's small windows. I'm right there with him. It won't be me, or morning sickness, shutting down the strut this time.

"It's just like waking up to a dream every morning," Ron says when I arrive. "We get a lot of morning wake-up calls from the birds banging around here."

That wake-up call comes when the sky turns from cold blue to warm orange. It's a male sage grouse adding volume to his vibe, the silky sound similar to the slow slide of legs wrapped in satin sheets. I bet that thin sweep of clouds swirling around those nearby peaks of the Centennial range makes the same smooth sound.

At the base of that range, an open stubble field sits close to the cover of a short sagebrush canopy. A seven-pound bird struts out from the brush into the clearing with a swollen chest, the source of that sliding satin sound. It's time to perform on the stage in the bar. This bird is looking for a dance partner.

"The males are trying to impress the females," Ron whispers with a gravelly chuckle. "Females walk by a male and he'll immediately start to display and try to get her attention, walking alongside her, and she just ignores him. Typical man-woman relationship."

We watch female grouse roll by glorious displays of fanned feathers and popping chests with little interest, just like girls ignore guys at bars. The rejection on repeat isn't mine, so it's an entertaining show. It's also a show that's getting harder and harder to see.

Leks are shrinking. The Idaho sage grouse population is down from an average of sixty males on a lek in 1959 to fifteen in 2009. Rumbles of the endangered species list bob in the Western wind like tumbleweeds.

Sage grouse need sagebrush year-round and through all stages of life. From mating and nesting, to food and cover, but sagebrush is going up in smoke. The brush is fast to burn and slow to grow.

Wildfires that used to spark every twenty-five years now light up every two to five years. Not nearly enough time for sagebrush to recover. Seedlings in a ten-year-old burn are only a foot tall. There's not enough food. Not enough cover. Not enough birds.

And yet, we can't force the future. I know this as I watch another female sage grouse avoid another male, and listen to Ron laugh quietly next to me. They really ought to mate for population's sake, but for some reason, well beyond my simple sense, they don't. The bar vibe turns pale, like bringing the lights up on the last song.

The male birds, desperate for a date, a second look, attention of any kind, expand their airbags again. Again with the sound of legs sliding along satin, this time followed by the pop of champagne corks. That's a quick airbag deflate for a repeat.

Another sound enters stage left. The beating of a drum. Two males are fighting. The drumming is their wings flapping frantically as they confront each other, a bar brawl with feathers instead of fists. They're fighting over who gets the girl, but she's not watching. No one gets lucky.

I'm thinking about what an endangered species listing means for ranching and recreation when the birds near our blind start to retreat. Early morning is turning late and they're seeking the safety of sagebrush. They'll wait out daylight and return to the lek's open area when the bar reopens at sunset for a repeat performance. Ron will be there. So will I.

"It's something everyone should have an opportunity to look at sometime in their life, because one day they won't be here," Ron remarks while we pack up gear and leave the birds to their business. "It's part of life. The good part of life."

A CENTURY OUTSIDE

SAGE GROUSE DON'T strut in fall like they do in spring. They stray. They're still partial to sagebrush, but choose thicker cover nowhere near that stage in the bar. They choose different land and they look different, too. The airbags sounding like satin sheets are gone. From far away, males and females look the same. Black spots the size of chickens.

I'm looking for those black spots in white snow while following an ancient Land Cruiser. We're in backcountry that is so far back, we passed the last dot on the map an hour ago. I know the ride in front of me is ancient because just as I flip my truck into four-wheel drive on the fly, brake lights blast my windshield. The Cruiser in front needs its hubs locked manually. I wait patiently. The driver needs no help from me and I'd rather avoid crawling around in the snow for a bit longer. We have a long, cold day of grouse hunting ahead of us in country stretching beyond comprehension.

"It's a big expanse of country you've got to see," Idaho hunter Chuck Cavanaugh had told me when he called me with directions to our rendezvous point. "I've lived here half my life and I haven't seen all the country yet."

I'm looking at the backside of Chuck's ride in the big expanse when the driver's door opens and a lean jean-clad leg swings out. I'm certain it's lean because it's attached to Chuck, the only hunter I know who weighs less than I do. Chuck is ninety-five in years and probably the same number in pounds.

I watch his bony, but far from fragile, frame squat at his rear tire, spin parts like an old bolt rusted in rain, then move to the next wheel to do the same. He's slight, but almost pit-crew fast in the pre-season snow. The white is too early, its flakes trying to steal the aspens' gold treasure. I admire the color contrast in the few minutes of wait, then we're back on the dirt road, cutting tracks in the cold blanket as we go.

Chuck spots large, chicken-sized bodies thirty minutes after the hub check. We park our vehicles. I have my video camera. Chuck has his 20-gauge.

The bird he's after is losing ground. As the sage grouse population shrinks, the hunting opportunity shrinks too. A few areas in Idaho still have a sage grouse hunt, but for most

hunters, the hunt isn't worth the gas it takes to get out. Most hunters aren't Chuck. He's still out, notably without a walking stick. At his age, he's as rare as the bird he's hunting.

"I don't care whether the bird gets it or not," he says, looking toward where he last saw birds settle in the snow. "So long as I have a good time."

His good time takes place in stunning scenery. Chuck himself is also stunning. Facial hair overruling standard beard boundaries, whiskers on his neck, in his ears, above his eyes. The details are lost, but not his dignity.

He has almost a century outside and he still spends 250 days a year in the hills. The only thing older than he is out here is the ridgeline north of us. His face is as weathered as the landscape, but his step is as sure as the sunrise. He credits fruit and fresh air for his endurance.

"It wasn't until I passed eighty that I got wise," Chuck says. "Eat right. No sugar at all. Fruit and vegetable diet with a little salmon will keep you going for years."

He leaves an apple lunch on the seat of his Toyota and walks out into the snow-dusted sagebrush with a pocketful of shells. In a simple jacket, the well-worn hunter loads his shotgun with wrinkled hands. His hunting partner is already out ahead of him. Chuck hunts with Jack Russell terriers, liking the way they sniff out grouse like a bloodhound hot on the scent of wild boar. I mentally note the dog's wiry coat matches Chuck's honest, wiry whiskers.

Roxy is a one-year-old terrier barely taller than the fresh layer of snow. She bounds like a bunny in the first fluff of the season, then suddenly stops and sticks her head in the snow. The wagging tail on her other end puts Chuck on alert. There are sage grouse in the brush. I watch with wonder as nature's great-grandpa steadies his stance in shin-deep snow and raises his shotgun. The desert birds flush. The historic hunter fires. The birds win the draw.

"I don't want more than one," Chuck says. "I hate to even shoot the one. I avoided one this time. I shot in the air past them."

One sage grouse, that's the bag limit where Chuck hunts. Fifty years ago he hunted the same ground and easily left with four or five birds.

"I have seen real heavy timber in this area years ago, and sage hens were thick. They were like a thundering cloud when they took off up here," he says as we follow the flushed feathers for another shot. "My first years up here there were very few hunters and hundreds of birds all around. When the fires come in, that terminated awful big bunches of birds."

Grazing in Idaho, drilling in Wyoming, and recreation across the West will be adjusted if sage grouse end up on the endangered species list. Something Chuck hopes doesn't happen before he's a hundred.

Chuck makes the four-hour drive for one bird at least three times during the hunt. He spends more than one hundred dollars in gas. He's shooting for five more years outside. And even though he's more miss than hit with his shotgun, the time and the expense are still worth it to him.

"Out in the hills every day don't hurt you a bit," he says, looking up to feel warm light leaking through the clouds.

Out in the hills with someone who's watched the wild for a century don't hurt you a bit either. We are birdless, but Chuck's a talker and I'm a listener. I roll while he reminisces. The red button on my camera has two modes: record and stop record. I push record and Chuck rambles. I let him.

The convenience of talking with people in record mode gives me an auto-out. When I'm done listening, I just hit the red button again to stop record, which also ends the discussion.

When people let their mouths run and I don't have a camera in my hand, I don't have stop record to cut the spew short. Outside of work, like at a party or on a plane, my endings wither. I've used record and stop record in conversations for so long that I've lost the ability to wrap an out-of-interview discussion politely. Sometimes I just want to yell "Stop record!" and walk away. I mean really, how else do I move on when mingling? You tell me. I'm stumped.

Awkward endings rattle my shy side, so it's unsettling when I can't stop record on a talker, but with Chuck, I don't want to stop record. He's more than double my age and I'm wishing for his wisdom. I hang on his every word like a rock star groupie about to sling something strappy onstage. Something that Chuck probably hasn't seen in decades.

UNDERESTIMATING
THE MIGHTY

WHILE CHUCK HUNTS birds on foot, Mike Griffin hunts birds by boat. Now I'm in his boat and I'm ashamed of myself. I underestimated the Mighty Mississippi and it took me a week to realize it.

I'm on assignment for the Izaak Walton League of America. I'm documenting what the Mississippi River means to the people who work and play along it. My home waters are, for the most part, void of pollution and full of trout. The Mississippi is nothing like that in my mind, so I'm not expecting beauty between its banks.

Yesterday a trapper told me we could use more muskrats and fewer eagles on the Mississippi. We almost had zero eagles when I was little, but he dismisses that. Last night I ate a lot of fried food for dinner, then stayed in a germ-gathering motel room with no lock on the door and blood splattered on the shower curtain. I say stayed instead of slept because I sat on my camera pack all night, not touching anything in the room and staring at the unlocked doorknob. Good thing I operate on little sleep.

I'm told there's redeeming beauty here, especially on the Upper Mississippi, but so far, what I see, hear, and eat is just as I expected: unappealing. I lived in southern Illinois for a little while when I worked for an ABC affiliate. Back when I flipped my hair up, wore skirt suits, and tried to anchor but never found my fit on the set. That's why I work outside now. It's where I fit.

Being back on this muddy red system where folks are Midwest friendly yet bumfuzzled, to borrow a Southern local's term, reminds me why I only stayed for a little while.

The Mississippi is a working river. *Overworking* is more precise. There's no union keeping its hours low and its value high. There's no limit on its use, and the strain of such a burden is barging through the Mighty like its supply is endless, but it's not. That's why I'm here. Like the Mighty Miss, I don't quit. I can't. Whatever is worth talking about here, I'll dig it up . . . starting with wildlife.

I spend an evening on the Miss with Jeff Janvrin during fall migration. He's a fisheries biologist for the Wisconsin Department of Natural Resources. He knows where to park his research boat for the best view of the show overhead. In the fall, everything that flies flushes up toward the nation's notorious flyway, the atmosphere's version of air traffic for whatever heads south ahead of winter. My lens is aimed at the sky as huge flocks float like a wave of arms started by fans in a football stadium. Jeff offers play-by-play of the action, then provides backstory like this waterway has a highlight reel.

"It is a river of commerce. It is a river of recreation. It is a river of inspiration," he says, skillfully steering his shallow vessel through stringy stems of marsh grass. "If we don't take care of this resource, what kind of message does that send to the rest of the world?"

I watch wings one night with Jeff and seek those wings the next morning with Mike. Mike's a duck hunter. Like Chuck, he hunts with dogs, but with Labs instead of terriers.

Mike's duck boat is piled so high with brush and tree limbs, I can't see through the leaves and grass to film. Sage grouse would hate this setup for their strut, but I keep at it. I'm running out of production days and I need to capture the assumed appeal of a place that so many sources rely on. Wildlife, industry, recreation. They all dip their ladle in the Mississippi, including the hunter I'm with now. He's one of the thousands of delighted hunters folding ducks in the fall from watercrafts sporting reeds and sedge as camo.

"I'm pretty proud of my boat," Mike says, navigating a backwater marsh.

He and his dogs are thrilled to be out. But I'm just tired. I've waited on first light and last light for five days. I've chased sediment sliding downstream and barges busting upstream. I've shot the water from above, on, and under. I've paddled canoes, hiked hills, smoked fish, and drunk plenty of hard cider in an effort to understand why everyone seems so fond of the Mississippi. I've listened and I've looked, yet my thoughts are still muddied by my preconceived notion of a worn-out artery twisted by human neglect.

Then Lilly, an eleven-year-old black Lab, pokes her head out of Mike's branch-buried boat. She has cataracts in her cloudy blue eyes. Though her view is murky, she proudly pops her head through the peephole, looking out over the water. I know she'll be the first to retrieve a duck should one fall.

Ash, an eighteen-month-old Lab, tries pushing Lilly out of the way, but she won't give. I recognize that trait. I studied it as a girl. Wanted it. Now, as a grown-up, I celebrate it. Don't give in or up. Ash won't have the duck boat's peephole until Lilly's done with the Mississippi. She performs as expected regardless of her cloudy eyes. She doesn't hide those eyes as a weakness, either, just figures out how to work with what she's got.

I stare at the aging dog with her gray muzzle. I'm admiring her feeble eagerness when my head clears like Lilly's eyes never will. Like Lilly, the river refuses to yield. For centuries, people have tried manhandling it—damming and directing it—but it won't tame, running proudly from Minnesota to Louisiana.

"The Mississippi is everything to everybody," Mike says, idling the boat next to recently restored bog. "This is the life-blood of America."

The Mississippi works for people, the industrial and the recreational kind. It also works for wildlife, the staying and the migrating kind. Its beauty is in its usefulness and in its ability to keep going.

Now I see the Mississippi. It took a duck dog with poor eyesight to show me, but now I really see it. Never underestimate the mighty whether it's a river, a dog or yourself.

FEEDING THE FIRE

DOC TELLS ME my leg is making enough progress for him, but it's not making enough progress for me. He's worried my patience with being a patient won't last. I'm worried about that, too. Frankly, I was better at sitting when I was passed out on pain pills. I'm not passed out anymore. I'm pissed off.

When the drug buzz fades, you realize how much time you have and you're doing nothing with it. Well, nothing you want to do, and what you have to do takes forever.

Do you know how long it takes to do anything injured? All the things we take for granted, doing them without thinking while clutter fills our heads. You have to clear that clutter to muster enough concentration for putting on one sock. One sock on one foot that seems frozen with time and titanium. It's exhausting, but being clutter free does bring clarity.

I use that clarity to come up with creative ways to do things. I've proven you can clip your toenails without bending your knee. Roll around on the floor for about an hour straining and stabbing with the clippers like a cat chasing nip. You'll catch a nail eventually, and that nail will catch on the sheets when you try to safely slide into bed.

Ooh, and this is a thrilling realization: convalescing is a lot like camping. You get out of your tent (bed), put on the same clothes you wore yesterday, brush your teeth (no other grooming required), and sit in a lawn chair (couch) by the fire (hearth) all day. See? Camping.

Exercise? Do it. You'll sweat while stretching your foot with that white dish towel you inherited from your grandma. She used it covered in fine, powdery flour while resting over rising bread. You use it covered in dead scraps of skin while rolling over your rumpled bones.

Sit-ups? Do them right after stretching and they're easy, easy when you have hours. All you have to do is slide from the couch to the floor, lie on your back, point the bad leg straight up toward the rafters like an old, rickety TV antennae, and flex your gut.

A pedometer sure would come in handy right about now, too. When the half bath runs out of toilet paper and you're home alone, you get to scoot clear down the stairs into the bowels of the basement for refill rolls. Do you know how far that is? There and back? Miles.

It takes me so long, I start looking for aid stations on the return trip, like the tables along racecourses where water is provided. By pedometer, I'm sure the steps I scoot tally high while I crutch extra slowly with two rolls of toilet paper, one squeezed between my sore armpit and the crutch top, the other pinched between my bruised palm and the crutch handle. The ordeal warrants a nap, but other than that I sit like I'm told. I do, but Doc and I both know it's a big ask.

My leg needs more time on the couch than I want to give it. I'm struggling to be in with something I don't want to look at because it means I can't go out. Out is where I feel my best, my most comfortable self. It's where I fit. I'm not comfortable on the couch, but at least this sit-in is happening while we're snowed in. If it had happened in summer, I would have figured out how to walk on my hands to get out of the house.

Right now this house needs heat. The couch where I currently live is on the main level. Heat rises to the second story, where the bedrooms are. I'm cramped and cold down here, so I crutch to the fireplace and light it with a switch, not a match. It's a gas fire, not a campfire. It's not a wildfire, either, but I've seen my fair share of those.

In some sadistic way, I like watching flame feed on forest because it's teaching us a hard lesson that's long overdue. Let me clarify before you balk. I don't like the death and destruction of fire. There's nothing to like about lives and livelihoods lost, but I do like the recklessness of fire's existence. It's wild, loose, out of the cage, beyond our control. Fire does its thing as intended so other things can do their thing as intended later. Fire, just like water, is a necessary natural resource element because it ignites new growth after smoldering.

That's what's represented in the square canvas to the left of my fish photo "Freedom." The square catches my eye as I crutch from the fireplace to the couch and settle myself on cushions and cubes of ice. I'm staring at "Make It" in the firelight. It's an image of a baby bird screaming for life without making a sound. Its mouth is open, but its cords aren't developed for chirping yet. My best guess is that it's a meadowlark, but it's so small that it's hard to tell. Maybe three days old.

I found this chick east of Rexburg, Idaho, the spring after a massive wildfire sprayed across the "big desert," as we around these parts like to call it, taking all the sagebrush and songbirds with it.

The "big desert" is a high-elevation environment. High as in 5,000 feet of elevation gain rather than the lowlands of Southwest desert that are much lower. High-elevation desert is still desert; it's just not movie desert.

Movie desert looks like sifted-fine cinder-colored sand and needle-drenched bosky-toned saguaros. The high-elevation desert of the West has cactus, too, but not picturesque saguaros with tall spines and full arms. High-elevation desert has short poke-your-ankles prickly pear cactus. It also has sagebrush and seasonal snow, but it's still a dangerously dry place. When winter wanes, the flames follow.

I covered a summer fire in the big desert, with its smoke filling life and lung, then returned the next spring to see what would happen next.

Upon return, I find the burn of black sprinkled with blades of emerald. Not sagebrush. No way. That'll take decades to come back, if it does at all. It's cheatgrass invading its way across the West as it does after every wildfire.

I move in measured steps, tripod in my left hand, camera in my right. The only sound I hear is my boots crunching spring's revival after last summer's death. I'm walking slowly, looking for life, and it's a good thing I am because I find it.

Meadowlarks are ground nesters, and a mama made its nest by swirling new shoots of green growth in a perfect cereal-bowl circle, creating a depression in the ground just large enough for three eggs.

All three have hatched, but only one will make it for sure. The one that ends up in the photo on my wall. That's the one that feels the vibration of my presence and pops up, head fuzzy, eyes blind, mouth gaping. It thinks its mom is here to feed it. The other two stay limp like my leg on the couch now, their necks not strong enough to trumpet upward yet. But when they are, their mom will feed them. When, not if.

STANDARD-ISSUE
STRUGGLE

THE BLEAKNESS OF fire isn't permanent, but it feels like it is when you're in the thick of it. It's similar to this struggle with my leg. It's not a permanent injury, but it sure feels like it is when I'm in the thick of it. Give anything a few months and it doesn't feel so thick, so permanent, anymore. I won't feel so vulnerable, so weak and exposed, when this ordeal is done.

Pregnancy takes a solid dose of time, too. Everything feels thick then, especially when you're trying to shove seven months of human incubation into pants made for men right before your first baby is due.

I was due in October when a fire lit up east of Idaho Falls in August. I was fire-certified media, so to the breaking scene I went.

I trained with the Idaho Falls Fire Department before wildfire season started. I crawled through a burning house wearing a fire suit, a face mask, and an oxygen tank. Just as movie deserts look different, fire behaves nothing like how you see it in the movies. You can actually see in movie fire—through the lens you always seem to have visibility. But in real-life fire, you can't see, especially in a house when the roof traps smoke until it collapses. A burning house has an extremely dark interior, even if it's burning during the middle of the day.

You can also hear in movie fire. You can't hear in real fire. The heated destruction is much too loud. If your earpiece falls out because you're sweating profusely inside your fireproof suit, you won't know where your crew is by sight or by sound. And you don't walk around, no. You crawl holding the leg of the crew member crawling in front of you. You search the floor for bodies on your hands and knees, feeling trapped in your suit in the hot dark. It's a terribly claustrophobic sensation. All you want to do is rip off your mask because you think you'll see better without it, but you won't breathe better. You'll suffocate instead.

That's a real house fire.

You can't see or hear in wildfire, either, but it smells and looks different. Wildfire smells like brush and bark instead of insulation and plastic. And wildfire always has its roof ripped

off, so the volume is immense. Several square miles of smoke and cinder easily disguise the scene unless the wind is in your favor for a brief flash, blowing the inferno away from you.

That wind helps me when the clothes I have to wear while pregnant don't. Wildfire clothes are the government's standard-issue burn-reducing uniform of yellow shirt buttoned up and tucked in, plus green pants on and zipped up. Tucked in and zipped up are mandatory. My laugh at such a mandate is also mandatory.

"Not happening," I tell the public information officer (PIO) before we leave for the August blaze.

"Then you're not going to the fire," the PIO responds.

"I'm going to the fire and I'm going untucked and unzipped. Here's why: this standard-issue outfit that's supposed to protect me isn't made for me. It's made for a man. I have hips, pregnant hips no less, and these man pants don't zip over woman hips or pregnant bellies. You make me tuck in this shirt and you're going to see all that is hanging out of my unzipped pants."

"We can't have that. No tuck, no zip, but you're staying farther from the flames than we originally planned."

"Deal. Now let's go."

I end up so far away from flame, I have to shoot the fire from one ridge over. Great for a wide shot, but you don't build a story with wide shots. That's too distant, too disconnected. To put an audience in the action rather than looking at the action, you need tighter shots. You need to be inside the action, where there are close-ups and medium-range shots, not all wide shots. You need to be in the fire, not watching it.

I'm not in it and that bugs me. I know the best way to capture a variety of shots is to hike over the calm ridge and onto the crazy one. The one where juniper is the burning bush and sage is the kindling. The one where lively orange eats the dull brown of the late season.

Needless to say, I'm let down by my location, but I have a remedy. You won't let me walk through fire untucked and unzipped, fine. I'll zoom through. I change my lens, adding a doubler, or telephoto lens. A doubler increases how far my lens can reach into the hot zone. Doubling my zoom doubles the depth I can create. I won't have close-ups of crackling fire, but I'll have medium and almost tight to add to the pile of wides I'm physically confined to.

The wind shifts to the south while I situate. From far away, I can see the whole burn and that thick smoke hiding sparks is about to roll with the wind. I'll see fire, not just smoke, when it does. I choose my target opposite of the wind direction and start recording as the breeze blows the plume away, clearing the scene.

I zoom in, way in, and what do I see through my lens? A yellow-top-green-bottom member of the fire crew. He's untucked and unzipped. He's peeing on the fire. He's in the heat of the action, so he doesn't know the wind lifted the smoke-concealing curtain. He doesn't know, but the pregnant, untucked and unzipped, reporter on the adjacent ridge knows.

I let out a mandatory, standard-issue laugh every time I think about that eye-opening moment.

SNORKELING FOR SALMON

MY LAUGHTER SUBSIDES as my thoughts drift to another fire assignment. This one involves fins. Humanity cripples watersheds with its heavy hand. Remove, reroute, run dry. We do this, then wonder why rivers abandon us when we need them the most, in wildfire season. A blaze burns through Idaho's Salmon River watershed annually. That's why black darkens both sides of the trail I'm hiking.

There's some new growth on the ground, but not much. Just acres of burned bark, bushes, and banks. I'm following researchers into a central Idaho drainage. The area is a wildfire hot zone. It's one of thirty-three crucial salmon survey sites. The crew is here to count fish. I'm here to see if they find any fish to count.

This crew is barely old enough to grow beards. I might be old enough to be their mom. It's the first time I'm the oldest person on a crew. My place is shifting, but I like where I am. I always knew what kind of woman I wanted to be when I grew up: shameless, not shy. But I wasn't born with the personality or the character traits to pull that off. I had to reprogram myself by learning to be what I wanted to be, and I chose to take my lessons outside. Shy took decades to shed, but being afraid of the dark ended after only one stormy night alone in a tent. I still have a slight germ phobia, but I abandoned my fear of beards by marrying one and working with many. Being able to talk to strangers, and know when to stop talking, I learned *that* outside, too. It's serving me well on the trail as I listen to the crew I might be old enough to mother.

We broke bread and the ice over dinner last night, so jokes are flying as fast as our feet are moving through the baked landscape. Dinner isn't sitting well with one of the guys carrying a scuba suit. I've named him Shitty Pants Shawn, and the thought of him trying to quickly unroll from tight rubber for a restroom emergency has us all in fits.

The only thing brighter than our attitudes is the pink fireweed flower breaking up the burn area. The color is sobering when you consider the other color at risk in this watershed. Red. Salmon red. We need to see salmon in here, but with so much black, the odds are bleak.

Wildfire is the way of the West during late summer, until the first significant snowfall. Smoke is the norm, while ashy air dominates lung capacity for weeks at a time as fire patchworks the forest and desert in a way man can't really control. We tried for decades. The result is untamed infernos blown up by Mother Nature, shaving off the scars of suppression from the let-nothing-burn era.

Most of us easily recognize land lost in a blaze. The huge expanse of dark cindered earth spreads as more and more of our undeveloped country bakes like a vicious urban sprawl, but black instead of build.

Water lost to fire is not as obvious as land loss. Life lost in that water is even less obvious. Rivers, streams, creeks. They can reach boiling potential in a wildfire: an unintentional fish fry. When the smoke settles, the snorkel crew goes looking for life in the dead landscape.

They're looking for native fish like cutthroat trout. They're also looking for salmon that travel more than eight hundred miles from the ocean to Idaho to spawn.

Salmon migration is a waterway wonder that intrigues me to no end. My persistence and intensity for this fish is frightening. My "no can't, no quit, just go" mantra intimidates others, yet I can't even begin to imagine what a salmon's pep talk must sound like. Talk about wild motivation: swim hundreds of miles, face impossible odds, then die for posterity and do it all with everything you've got. Salmon are saints. Endangered saints. And because of that, the crew has to count fish without laying a finger on them. That's why they snorkel, with Jordan Messner as their lead counter. He's another one of Idaho's biologists. He specializes in fisheries, and in central Idaho that means sensitive salmon species. They're supposed to be in this drainage fighting unbearable odds.

"When you're in some of that really turbulent water, really high-velocity water, it's trying to rip your mask off your face and rip your snorkel out of your mouth," Jordan says, zipping his wetsuit snug up to his hooded face. "It'll plug up your ears real quick. It can get pretty loud, so we have hand signals we use to relay counts to the data recorder on the bank."

I'm doubtful there's any data to record as the wet-suited counters start crawling upstream with their snorkel-covered faces in the water. I settle on my wader-covered knees in the current, my camera on the ready and in record mode. I have to hold still so I don't stir up ash ahead of the team.

I'm usually an optimist, but floating in funeral hues is depressing and I favor pessimism as they move single file across the creek in a slow sweep. I drove across the state for this morbid scene? There's no way there are freshwater trout in this burn area, let alone saltwater salmon from several states away.

A few minutes pass, and I think I'm the know-it-all. I am the eldest. These young punks are trying to fit my scene. Then two hands pop out of the water with eight fingers up. Eight fish swim by; their fin flips prove I'm wrong. I love it when the wild proves me wrong. There is life in this water.

"You stick your face underwater and start crawling up the stream and there's way more fish in there than you thought," Jordan says with his mouth barely above the current. "You can watch them feed a lot of times. Just kind of watch them do their thing."

While they do their thing, I do mine. I work from above the water, but also drop a lens under the water. I only have one day with this snorkel crew, so I'm going for every angle I can muster. I capture footage of the underwater rock climbers creeping over the length of two football fields. They form a line three men across from bank to bank. Moving against the current is taxing, even on sturdy bodies built for this kind of work.

"It's a workout for sure," Jordan says while kneeling in the water to take a breather. "It will kick your butt."

The snorkelers, doing their water workout, keep count as fish fins pass their rubber flippers. I should know better than to doubt the resilience of the natural world when it comes to recovering from fire. The count includes salmon, steelhead, and bull trout, along with many other non-endangered fish like cutthroat trout.

Soaked but smiling faces get out at the end of the wet run. The healthy tally reveals a successful count—and no emergency bathroom breaks for our sickly swimmer, Shitty Pants Shawn.

We pack up and move on in haste. Midsummer snorkeling days are fifteen hours long, but no one is watching the clock. There's a lot of current to crawl through, and it's worth seeing while the sun shines.

LET IT FLOW

NOT FAR FROM the snorkelers is another drainage, the Yankee Fork. It's the kind of drainage miners like instead of snorkelers. It's the kind of drainage humanity's heavy hand wiped off the map for the love of money. Now it's costing even more money to put it back. This I gotta see. Up close, on my belly.

That's where I am when I have one of those moments. You know the kind: a moment of such clarity that you must stop busying, and settle. It happens often when I'm on video shoots that involve wildlife in wildlands. It's an astounding sensation, experiencing one of these moments. Awkward in their arrival, but where I fit best. An unexpected expedition. I attach to these moments every time one presents itself, and this one . . . oh, this one is remarkable.

It's a moment so divine, I stop working to stare. I know in the back of my mind that my camera is still recording, but at the forefront, I'm witnessing a miracle as an angler rather than as a reporter. Here, belly down on a beaver dam, I see for the first time what most people will never see in their lifetimes—an endangered Chinook salmon swimming the last leg of its 850-mile journey from the Pacific Ocean to Idaho to spawn. Cassi Wood is with me when I see my first Chinook. She's Trout Unlimited's Central Idaho project specialist and she's one of the many minds behind what makes salmon sightings possible. I admire her. She's slight in stature, but weak in no obvious way. She has the vigor and might I followed when I was her age but have since learned to lead with. Finding your own fit does that.

"As soon as the fish come in, you know you've done something right," Cassi says as my underwater camera records the fishery.

Trout Unlimited and the U.S. Forest Service, along with about a dozen other funding partners, are putting the Yankee Fork of the Salmon River back together—a river that was turned upside down and inside out seven decades ago for gold. And for good reason according to Rich Allen. He's president of the Yankee Fork Gold Dredge Association (YFGDA). He spends summers in the old dredge camp. He tells it like it was, matter-of-fact.

"When mining started in 1940, it was right after the Depression and before World War II. Men needed jobs. They were at the dredge camp," Rich says as I interview him by his camp trailer above the mine site. "Granted, they don't do that anymore, but that's what happened in those days and it was acceptable."

The days Rich refers to are the decades of resource extraction for the sake of western expansion and the industrialization of our nation. In the early 1900s, Americans wanted the natural world for what they could get out of it (wood, minerals, hydropower) versus what they would gain by leaving it as it was (trees, meadows, creeks).

Many of the acceptable practices from days gone by shaped the scarce situation salmon are in today. They face unbelievable odds migrating to and from the ocean. That's why most of them never live to see another spawning bed after they leave their native one.

On their return migration, only a few dozen make it all the way to the Yankee Fork near Stanley, Idaho, in the fall. Thankfully, every fall, the seven miles of dredge tailings in their way—the massive mounds of waste rocks left over after miners sifted through it for gold—shrinks.

That's the fix. The fix started in 2012. Slow but steady sectional repairs to the river are done in phases annually during the area's short warm season. The Yank is a cold and shady place. The water is even colder. Construction season is limited.

The loud beep of heavy machinery moving in reverse only bounces off the choppy ridges for a few snow-free weeks in the late summer and early fall. That's when workers restructure ponds into channels and reconnect tributaries by using bulldozers to move tailings. Helicopters also drop timber for fish cover as the flow finds its place again.

One construction zone at a time, the Yankee Fork is behaving more like what it was made for rather than what it was mined for. Otters, beavers, mountain goats, deer, steelhead, and salmon are making their presence known with the return of the waterway. Results are encouraging, but not everyone likes what's going on.

"I think it's a waste of money," Rich says, looking at the rock piles, the tailings. "I'd leave the tailings. No question. That's what this valley is about. This valley is about mining. It's not about fishing. Why destroy this for a couple of fish? You'll never convince me that what they're doing down there is advantageous compared to how much money they're spending."

I don't convince. I don't have to. My job is to let each side speak, and speak Rich does. I don't waste words. Neither does Rich. He represents the more than one hundred members of the YFGDA. Some are mining families; others are friends of Idaho's rich mining heritage. The old gold dredge they revere is still in the Yankee Fork and it's parked on Forest Service property, but the association runs the daily tours.

Around eight thousand visitors filter through the historic site between Memorial Day and Labor Day. The tailings, the result of collecting about $1 million in gold in an area estimated to hold $16 million, are part of the tour. Heaping stockpiles of relocated stone fan out across the original abandoned riverbed like waves made of rock instead of water. Those waves are known as windrows, and restoration wipes out windrows for, as Rich says, a couple of fish.

His stance is strong, but so is Cassi's. To her, a couple of fish are certainly worth it. The struggle between Rich and Cassi is my story. As a reporter, my opinion on the matter doesn't matter. Rich's does. Cassi's does. And I'm sorting their sides while watching a rare fish when I meet Lafe Gamett.

Lafe is eleven years old and he smells like outside, just like my boys do. He's observant and keen, with a fresh face still many years away from a beard. He's watching from the bank as I lie on the beaver dam, collecting fish footage. He quietly points to where my lens is aimed, and I know we're both enthralled with the same thing: the silent swimmer from the sea.

"I think it's really cool how the fish roll around and pat their tails to put the rocks out of their way," Lafe says.

The particular spawner Lafe and I are watching is in a bad way. The rocks below its belly are rubbed clean and covering eggs. Life cycle complete, the salmon is still standing guard on probably the last day of its life. Its fins are threadbare. Its scales are nearly colorless. Its condition is much like my grandpa's in the nursing home. His eyes are open and he's moving around, but his skin is stale and his mind is wandering.

Sometimes I carry my grandpa's old fishing license with me when I fish, hoping some of his younger spitfire will bring me luck and eyes-up courage. Or maybe if I stand in the water long enough, the swirling sensation around my calves will transfer to his aged, aching feet.

There's nothing more humbling than realizing your own mortality through the disintegration of a grandpa you grew up idolizing as stalwart. The same holds true for old fish, especially salmon and their epic journey. It's a marvel to me, and yet they're not graceful. But they serve their purpose thoroughly until their dying day. Did the miners of my grandpa's era see salmon as they turned the river upside down seventy years ago? And what about Lafe? Will he, and my own boys, see salmon when the Yank is put back together seventy years from now? What if Lafe was Lafe the miner's son instead of Lafe the fish biologist's son?

"Certainly, fish is one of the big reasons we're engaged in this effort, but really what we're doing is restoring a watershed," says Lafe's father, Bart Gamett, U.S. Forest Service fish biologist. "That means clean water. It means a better place for people to come to recreate, and overall, a healthier system that we'll leave to future generations."

That's why what I'm capturing on camera, as I hold in prone position on top of the beaver dam, matters. We need rivers that run so the fish living in them can run, too.

I hold with reverence as the dying yet defensive Chinook swims toward the logs I'm lying on. It can't see me with only one working eye left, but I keep myself, and my wading boots, clear of the waterline anyway. There's a redd, its spawning bed, a few yards upstream of me. I don't want my feet anywhere near that fish's future. Those eggs are precious. The Chinook is protecting life while on its deathbed. The scene, a struggle infused with serenity, stills me like nothing else can and stays with me like nothing else ever will.

"This is really important," Lafe says. "We need fish in order to have our world go around right."

Agreed. We also need the water they live in, the food they provide, and the family bonds we reinforce while wading through their streams with Grandpa's old fishing license in our pocket.

WHERE THE GOATS GO

I HAVE A few cover-worthy images that go beyond my walls and onto the front covers of magazines. One of those is "Gruff." "Gruff," as in "The Three Billy Goats Gruff" fairy tale, is a vertical shot of a mountain goat on a small outcropping swallowed by dense forest in all directions. It decorated the cover of *East Idaho Outdoors* magazine a few summers back. I like the photo, but I hate goats. No, scratch that. I hate Hendricks. Nope, still not enough venom. I despise goats and Hendricks and I'm verbal about it as I chase both.

Hendricks, first name Curtis. Remember him? The guy who tackles deer and loses cameras? Yeah, him. He's tracking a mountain goat now, and I'm tracking him. We're close in age, with a lot of know-each-other years between us. I've seen him single, married, divorced, and trying to date. He's seen me stressed, mad, delirious, and trying not to look desperate.

He's looking for a mountain goat wearing a radio collar. That collar is sending a mortality signal. When a collar doesn't change location for a span of hours, the signal changes, indicating there's a problem. It means there's a dead goat in the rough and rocky ridges between Idaho and Wyoming. Or it means an animal slipped its tracking chokehold, and a collar is

randomly lying in unfriendly country somewhere higher than the tree line, around ten thousand feet above sea level, give or take. Either way, Curtis is trailing mountain goats and I'm trailing Curtis because I want to see mountain goats. I wish I didn't *want*.

Mountain goats hang out where humans shouldn't, especially humans with cameras and tripods. It's too bad I don't give up, because right now I really want to. My gear is heavy and Curtis is quick on our steep roadless route. We are four hours in, and the only reason I'm still in is because my lunch is in Curtis's pack. He's dangling it like a carrot while waiting well ahead of me. The dangling and the waiting really piss me off. If he's waiting, that means I'm not moving fast enough. But I don't move fast when I'm hangry.

I fantasize about the knuckle sandwich I'd like to give him. I'm going to need a lesson in patience after this. My frustration reveals itself and I holler, "We have to stop. I'm not in a good place mentally."

Curtis hollers back, "You're saying you're not in a good place mentally and I'm saying we're not in a good place physically. We're down here and we need to be up there."

"Screw up there!" I yell with delirious desperation. "I want my lunch down here!"

Curtis concedes and comes down, and we eat before I blow a gasket. My PB&J sandwich is not as tasty as the knuckle kind I want to give Curtis, but it will do. My time is coming. Curtis is creepy fast while in pursuit, but I am creepy good at glassing ridges with my naked eye.

I'm scanning while I fill my gut with food. I spy white moving two ridges away. Curtis uses optics to confirm I'm not hallucinating. I'm hangry, but I'm not hallucinating. There really are goats clear over there.

We watch from very afar while we eat. I wish I were a thief. I would steal Curtis's lunch and his trekking poles. But not his antenna—that's cumbersome. He can keep that. He needs it to pick up the signal we're after anyway.

"Radio collars answer a lot of questions," he says around a mouthful of not-so-knuckle sandwich. "We are able to lift the lid a little bit on animal behavior and how they move on the landscape."

After lunch, we spend an hour picking our way through a huge bowl of scree at the midsection of a sword-sharp peak that if it could talk would say, "Turn back or die." The scree field is so massive, we look like tiny pebbles rolling around in a weatherworn impression larger than one hundred Olympic-size swimming pools full of thin loose sheets of rock that slip like a heap of broken dinner plates. I'm going to need new boots after this.

It takes an hour to scramble up another ridge to a point that puts us above the herd. There's no hurry with all of this. The billies and nannies don't have anywhere else to be unless we push them, but we've worked too hard to push them.

"I think that's part of the appeal that keeps me coming back to the alpine country," Curtis says, closing the antenna and getting ready to crawl. "You get up here and it's so big, it's amazing. A lot of vertical, a lot of exposure, and you can see a long ways. It's incredible country."

He's right about that, and I'm incredibly spent when I abandon upright and start crawling toward the cliff one-handed, the camera in my other hand. The plan is for me to quietly poke my head and camera over the edge to spy on five mountain goats foraging below. Goats like to run upward when they flee. Upward is me. They won't have anywhere to go, so if I'm reverent and nonthreatening, they'll stay put.

Curtis is biologically brilliant in the ways of the wild, camera mishaps aside. That's why I like to shadow him when he works. I know this plan will work, because he came up with it. Belly crawl begins. I'm going to need a new vest after this.

The stealth plan works and I get my first up-close visual with audio added. Goats are noisy. They snort, burp, and chew with their mouths open. The sounds are surprising, and I'm showing a toothy grin when I give Curtis my *Yes, I'm getting all of this* nod.

"They're putting all their groceries on their back in the summer," he whispers. "Then they'll hunker down and live up here through winter."

I definitely won't be here in the winter, but I'm here now and one of the goats knows it. It looks at me for a long time. I look back. Wouldn't it be neat to know how it describes me? Here's how I describe it: white coat tinged with yellow, especially on the lower jaw, where long wisps of light strands swing with the goat's chewing motions. The longer that billy goat's gruff, the more it swings like a waterfall. Below that coarse cascade of beard are these crazy feet—hooves, actually. Softer than acceptable hooves for the terrain. And back at that mouth, absolutely unacceptable table manners.

But who cares about their manners? This is their home. They can eat how they want and I'll watch. Forget about pushed patience, trashed boots, and a ruined vest. I'm hanging over a cliff with a camera, watching the wild. The really wild. The rarely-if-ever-sees-humans wild.

Never mind what I said earlier about hating goats. I really like goats, but Curtis, aka Hendricks, is already telling me we're losing light. It's time to go. I still hate Hendricks.

GROPING A GRIZZLY

CURTIS AND I knock heads, but it's friendly. I say I hate him, and in certain situations, like when he loses my camera or holds my lunch hostage, I really do hate him, but it doesn't last. Our friendship is stronger than those blips. With bear biologist Bryan Aber, there's no friendship, at least not for the first few years while he avoids me. It's not because I'm a woman; a lot of his field technicians are women.

It's because I'm a reporter. Bryan doesn't trust the media. Not an original excuse, but it's what he's using. I hate getting lumped in with the "media" pile as someone not to trust. I know who I don't trust and I make sure I don't match their traits, but Bryan doesn't know that. Not at first.

He watches me work with other biologists for a few months. He watches my stories for plenty more months and then finally decides I have skills. I'm in. So I let the trust start to build with the man sporting a beard as prickly as his personality. Despite that, we connect. I'll ask you to take off your sunglasses during an interview so the audience can clearly see your eyes and make a more intimate connection with you as a person, but I don't need you to lose the beard so I can connect. Beards don't bother me anymore. Not even Bryan's. I've earned my place in the woods with him, which has me hearing my mom in my head again.

"You really should be more careful," she would say, with sky-is-falling worry forever in her eyes. *"You take too many risks. I swear you don't have a danger gene."*

In this instance, I'm thinking she's wrong. I must have a danger gene. Why else would my hand hover over a pelt with a shaking tremor reaching all the way to my fingertips? I'm hesitating, but honestly, any sensible soul would pause when put in my position. I'm in the far back of the backcountry with a grizzly bear, and our run-in is no accident.

"There's really a small number of people worldwide who work with these species," Bryan says. "It's a pretty cool thing to be part of that and help recover the population in the Greater Yellowstone Ecosystem."

He's letting me in on his cool thing. I'm with him when he traps a grizzly bear in a dense forest of lodgepole pine in Island Park, Idaho, just outside of Yellowstone National Park. I'm witnessing one day in two decades of grizzly bear research in the

GYE. We traveled a dizzying maze of dirt roads to reach the trap. I wouldn't be able to find it on my own if I tried, but the site is marked a mile out with signs reading DANGER. DO NOT ENTER. Only a handful of people know what goes on behind the signs, and I'm with them.

I'm nervous, a reporter at a grizzly bear trap site. That's unheard of. I'm giddy. I've always wanted to touch a grizzly bear without losing my life. That's also unheard of, but I have to keep my head in the game or Bryan will kick me out before I adjust to being in. I'm going along to tell the story of the science behind the bears through video and photo.

Grizzlies landed on the endangered species list about the same time bald eagles did, but I never saw a grizz in my school gym. This is my first time, and I intend to touch that bear, but there's plenty of work to do before that hovering hand holds wild hair.

As I unload my cameras, we talk in whispers. The wind is still. The woods around the trap are quiet until a rumble rises. The noise sounds like an idling car buried in snow. The sound spreads from the trap, through the trees, to the trucks vibrating my tripod. It's the growl of a grizzly. I lean in for a look through the bars on the trap's window. The grizzly throws a paw at the opening with a loud bang. I jump a lot and pee a little.

I'm uncomfortably close, but I don't back away and I don't look away. This is my first grizzly. I study it, staring wide-eyed with my too-close eyes that don't seem so close anymore. I lasted longer in the media business than the news director who made that ridiculous remark about my eyes way back when, so I don't fret over my facial features anymore. I'm comfortable with me, including the quirks I carry. Quirks, kinks, hitches, hang-ups. We all have them. It's best if we learn to shoulder them with dignity if they're going to stay despite how far behind we try to leave them.

The animal I'm staring at has a quirk too. He's a sucker for an easy meal. That's why he's in a trap. Meat enticed him to enter. Now I'm enticed to stare at him. The moment needs no soundtrack, so my long ago too-quiet voice doesn't need a shot of whiskey for volume, but my nerves might need one for soothing.

The experienced researchers are looking at the same grizzly I'm looking at. It's not their first, but it's significant nonetheless. It's Grizzly No. 227, the first grizzly captured for research in modern-day Idaho. That was back in 1994, when the population was close to blinking out. No. 227 likes rotten elk meat. He's been baited into a trap twelve times in twenty years.

"That's kind of impressive," Bryan says after tranquilizing the bear. "He's a twenty-one-year-old bear now, and it's kind of cool to see how he's gone through the years."

Once the bear settles into a drug-induced sleep, the team works quickly. They pull 440 pounds of bear out of the trap, put him on oxygen, and start collecting hair and blood samples. They have forty-five minutes to collect what they need and put a new GPS collar on No. 227. I have the same amount of minutes to shoot video, take photographs, and sneak in the touch I'm itching for.

It took me five years of solid storytelling to prove myself worthy of this bear-trapping trip. I'm thrilled to work with Bryan, even when he rolls his eyes at me as I lie down on the tarp next to him. His hands are in the bear's mouth, and my hands are all over my camera.

"Really, Millgate?" he whispers.

I whisper back, "You do your job, I'll do mine."

The rapport between us is stern, but well developed over our common interest. Bryan knows bears like no other, and as a journalist it's my job to know the know-it-alls. I watch Bryan manhandle teeth in the bear's mouth, then move to its neck to tighten screws on the new GPS collar. Hair samples are pulled. Blood is drawn.

During all of this, I fight the light. Light is tricky at a trap site. A camera lens, no matter how much it costs, doesn't literally work like your iris. It adjusts based on how much light there is, but it gets confused by how much light there is when the light source is patchy.

Grizzly trap sites have less than favorable lighting conditions because they're always in the shade. Hairy grizzlies overheat easily, so working on an unconscious bear in directly overhead sun for nearly an hour could mean death by heatstroke for the animal. The work has to be done in the shade. Even in the shade of a tight growth of lodgepole pine trees, light is patchy, especially when the wind blows branches and sun sprinkles through. Just beyond that patchy light, our small square of working shade is immediately swapped for full sun. I'm always looking for full shade or full sun, but not both at the same time or half of each. That confuses the lens and creates shots that are either too dark or so overexposed that they look blown out with a white glow.

The bear's life has priority over the life of my shot, so I continue to fight the light as inspection of the beast continues. There's an ugly wound from a recent bear fight that's repairing itself naturally with a mound of maggots. The old scar from a hunter's gunshot in 2009 is still trouble free. No. 227's teeth are wearing down. His weight is down, too. He's aging. This is all documented before the bear's sleepy-time tranquilizer runs out.

The medicine wears off from nose to toes. The bear is starting to lick his lips. Time's up and my shaky hand is still hovering. The research crew quietly jokes about my hesitation. I quickly bite back, reminding them we are all kneeling around something that could kill us with one paw swipe.

Finally, I dismiss the danger like my mom says I always do, and go for a grab of grizzly, no whiskey courage needed. The omnivore's course coat is deep, dense, and dirty. Just as for little boys on summer vacation, baths are optional for big bears, too.

I run my hand along the huge hump between the bear's shoulders. His breathing is extremely slow and deep. The calm, restful state of such a powerful brute is unsettling.

This beast of a bear lives where I do, he swims the rivers I fish, and he eats the berries I pick. He doesn't really want to be anywhere near me. I feel the same about him when he's awake, but for this one moment we are both harmless. His hair is covered in dandruff and dirt. It's wildly fierce, but I enjoy the feel of it like it's the finest fabric I've ever run my fingers across.

"He's walking around out here and he could pretty much have anything in there," Bryan jokes.

That's his way of telling me time's up, stop touching. I pull my hand free, stand up, and step away. Grizzly No. 227 is lifted back into the trap. Bryan cleans up the outdoor operating room, then runs a rope-and-pulley system from trap to truck. This is how he'll open the trap at sunset, so the bear can run off with its new GPS collar, leaving the trap empty for the next unsuspecting bear.

"The grizzly bear population has recovered and should be delisted," Bryan tells me while we're sitting in the truck, waiting for the bear to wake up. "It's a good feeling to be part of that."

Witnessing that recovery is a good feeling, too. There were fewer than two hundred grizzly bears in the GYE when they landed on the endangered species list in 1975. I was two years old. They left the list in 2017 with more than seven hundred grizzlies in the GYE, but they were relisted in 2018, so I'm still following their story.

As we drive away from Grizzly No. 227, the trapdoor opens. Another collared grizzly bear runs out of the trap and out of sight. I've had my once-in-a-lifetime touch-a-grizzly moment. My hands are still shaking. Touching a grizzly, even a sleeping one, will do that to you.

GROPING A GRIZZLY AGAIN

THAT ONCE-IN-A-LIFETIME TOUCH turns into two touches, and I'm nose to nose with a grizzly again. Crazy Curtis is in charge of this operation. We started early. He didn't shave and I use his stubble to refine my focus. He has no idea how many times I've zoomed in on him over the years, zeroing in on what makes him fit, like I used to do to people I studied in my shy-hide little-girl way. My lens finds the finest focus on his face, then I adjust the angle for something more intimidating, an animal that can kill me with one claw.

But it won't because the bear is out cold. The four-year-old male grizzly is under the spell of a sleepy-time shot so researchers can examine him. Sounds like a bucket list assignment, right? Hang on. Honestly, it stinks. The stink is rotting fish guts dripping down the tree trunk behind me and sun-cooked roadkill elk steaming in the dirt next to me. I dry heave violently with my back to the biologists. I have a sensitive nose. My sniffer is always in overdrive, but this crew doesn't need to know about my excellent sense of smell. That's a distraction.

I push the smell away and pull my skills close. It works and I only gag when no one is looking.

Wild meat in summer heat is a wretched odor rivaled only by the unbathed scent of dirty bear. Flies are feasting on the rotten fare and so was the bear until the shoulder poke that put it down with its claws out. This bear isn't in a trap, just a leg snare. Grizzly No. 1,225 is not as desperate for meat as Grizzly No. 227 and he's smarter than the boxy human contraption on wheels. He sniffs around the door, but never enters. The cable around the tree next to the trap holds his leg tight instead, leaving him on full display.

I see every part of this beast except his eyes. Those are closed. The steady in-and-out rhythm of his breathing is mesmerizing, and I relax into my shooting routine. I fill frame with his shoulder hump for the first shot. Next shot, claws. I can't help myself. Those deadly, flesh-ripping daggers grab my attention every few seconds. I have a lot of claw shots.

Shot three, the rising of his body on a deep intake of air that sounds like a snore. Match that sleeping action with a shot of closed eyes for number four in the sequence. It's during shot four that the scene explodes and so does my bladder.

I always hold steady on every shot for at least ten seconds so I have some pad to work with in the edit bay. About halfway through my steady hold on shot four, the bear's closed eyes open.

Startled, I yank my face away from my camera as if I've captured the scene wrong mechanically and I need to assess with the eyes in my head instead of the lens in my hand. The bear follows my lead and lifts his head.

"He's up!" I say loudly. "He's really up."

I raise my upper body by extending my arms. The bear copies my motion. At this point, I turn into a four-year-old, too. I want, with all my heart, to play follow the leader. If I stand, the bear will stand, so let's not do that. Let's lie back down and close our eyes.

I fold my arms and flatten my body onto the same tarp the bear is sprawled on. The bear doesn't follow my lead. I'm down and he's still up, head bobbing, tongue rolling, nose sniffing. He jerks hard to relieve his nostril of the oxygen tube, then sucks in deeply to get a good whiff of me, the girl who smells like fear and pee.

"Hey!" I say. "He's definitely up. Can I get up?"

I'm too close to a bear that's too awake. This isn't how this is supposed to go. I can only be at the trap site when the bear is knocked out. He's not out, but I'm in.

The crew knows I'm not bluffing. Everyone starts moving—everyone but me. I should rise and run to the truck, with my camera of course, but the bear is keyed in on me. Curtis leans close to my ear and says, "I know you're a runner. Don't run."

He rushes to the truck in twelve paces, fills a syringe, and beelines for the backside of the bear in another dozen steps. The moment is more intense than claws out. It's that visceral instant when lucidity is about to swing from woman to wild.

I have no control over the volatile situation. That shatters my resolve, but I won't let it kill my confidence in a man who I casually call crazy but instinctively I trust. Years of working together in uncomfortable situations creates connections no bear, or beard, can break.

With Curtis about to medicate the rousing grizzly, my body doesn't move, but my eyes dart between bear and bark. The bear isn't mobile yet, but when he is, that leg snare wrapped around the tree trunk, looking about as strong as dental floss wrapped around a tooth, will snap. I just know it. And it's the only thing keeping the beast at bay. Bark is going to fly when the bear totally comes to. I bet we both break eye contact then. Don't blink.

The deadly staring contest continues. He's studying me. Does he see weakness, threat, bravery, or hysteria? He has to be as uneasy about what's going on as I am. Maybe more so. He has to be. Nothing about this close encounter is comfortable to settle into. Not now. Not ever, but here we are, bellies flat, gazes locked. Him wondering what I am. Me wondering when Curtis will strike. One of us is held by man's snare. The other, by self-dare. Can't exactly say which I am—maybe both.

I stop wondering when I hear Curtis inhale deeply above me and I feel the bear exhale directly at me. I don't inhale or exhale. I've stopped breathing. Stopped moving. I'm frozen by death at my door . . . in my face, really.

With another dose of drowsy delivered, control of the scene slowly sways back to human and I never see bark fly. The bear's consciousness fades before he has me figured out. Eyes never averting, just lids lowering. Looking away or hiding won't get either of us out of this situation, so I hold my stare, too, until total shutdown. Curtis leans close to my ear again and, to break the insanely intense moment, says, "Told you he was asleep."

We return at dusk. Grizzly No. 1,225 was passed out when we put him in the trap to sleep off his double dose of hangover. Younger bears metabolize medicine faster than older bears. In some cases, much faster. That's what happened here when I faced an eyeful of fatal attraction.

Now Grizzly No. 1,225 is sitting up in the trap. I see him through the bars, head hanging down, eyes averted, but alert without looking at us directly. I know that look; I wore it well in my younger days. It's submission. It's fear, fear of dark places and bearded faces, among many other things. It's hesitation. It's hide with a hint of *Get me out of here now.*

It's also *I can't believe you're looking at me in this condition. This is not who I really am. I am wild. I am free. At least I will be as soon as you open that door and let me run from this embarrassing situation.*

I've learned to embrace embarrassment. I'm not expecting a wild animal to do that—we shouldn't attach human behavior to what isn't human. But that look is unmistakable. The bear doesn't fit with us. The bear knows it. The bear wants out and it's never coming back. He's learned his lesson, just like I have. Fitting in is not for the free-spirited.

UNFINISHED BUSINESS

THERE ARE JOKES about being the fastest runner in the group when camping in bear country. I spend a lot of time in the woods, so I'm determined to be the fastest, or at least the person who can run the farthest. That's why I run long distances on trails. I ran nearly one thousand miles last year. With my leg in recovery mode, I'll consider myself lucky if I run one mile this year.

My quads at the peak of trail-running season are a toned twenty inches each. Now my left quad is down to seventeen inches; my right quad is fifteen inches. I feel sorry for myself. Yuck. But it's not permanent. I have to keep reminding myself of that. Surprisingly, this isn't my lowest point. Going no place is bad, but last place is worse, much worse.

When I'm in last place, I stink more than a grizz does, but it would still eat me. Bears like stink, and I stink in last place like I stunk on that 108K trail race in 2016. I was at the back of the pack. Easy takedown. Easy meal.

I was dead last.

Me, the ever-prepared, can't-quit overachiever, in last place. Are. You. Kidding. Me? It's so unbelievable, I'm as numb to the reality of my plight as I am to the bubbling, bleeding blisters

on my heels. They started at mile five. I'm on mile twenty-five somewhere above ten thousand feet in central Idaho wilderness.

Enter my world, but make it quick for your own sake. The mental madness of reporter versus runner is only tolerable in tiny doses.

Reporter: Blisters?

Runner: I'm not talking about blisters. I'm talking about the pain of this midlife crisis tightly squeezing my fragile cocoon of self-confidence.

Reporter: Speaking of tight, your feet are stepsister swollen in Cinderella's soiled slippers. Lack of water is the problem. So is lack of food. You're burning twice as many calories as you're eating, yet you're still moving. How is that even possible? It doesn't make sense.

Runner: The clouds don't make sense. Why are they moving so fast? Or am I moving that slowly? I'm wondering and wandering. I mean, running.

Reporter: Why do you run?

Runner: I run to reach the far-flung places I'm expected to report on. Not being physically fit enough to reach a story would be mortifying, so I run to make sure I'm trained for anything. At first, it was just three miles. But somehow three turned into thirty. Now running feels more like my job than reporting does.

It's extreme, and extreme isn't what my parents expected out of me, but I'm no longer the girl they raised. I've made damn sure of that. It's not that I rebelled, but rather I evolved. I love them, but I will amount to more than just a product of them. My adventures astound my parents and my siblings, my decisions intimidate them, my goals outweigh them, and my risks scare them. But how do you really come to know yourself without taking risks? I choose extreme risk, extreme living—and the deeper into the wild I go, the better. There's no pretense out here when you're stripped to your core, laid bare by the wild. To be this vulnerable, to strip away others' expectations, is freeing.

My sister once asked me, "What are you running away from?"

"I'm not running away," I confidently replied. "I'm running to."

Reporter: To what?

Runner: To work. I mean, to water. Ooh! A creek!

Reporter: Are you sure? The last water you nearly jumped in was a sagebrush sea mirage.

Runner: It's babbling. It's real. I'm babbling, but I'm coherent enough to know I can't drink it. Hey! I can certainly soak in it.

Reporter: Yes, feet, rule the delirium. Step in. We've all tried so hard today. We deserve a soak, but only for two minutes.

Runner: I soak in wading boots. I run in them, too. I run downstream with a zinger on the line, run out of the willows with a moose on my tail, and run back to the truck for my fishing license. All runs done in wading boots. Desperate runs, but runs nonetheless.

This is a desperate run, too. A run in a rugged place that's undeveloped, unforgiving, and unwelcome for the sissy-footed. I'm running what most people won't walk. Go, girl! Well, I was running until this snow-fed creek crossed my path and my oozing heels forced me to ease up and wade in.

Reporter: You're wading in water that holds fish. You wanna fish instead?

Runner: I wear a bandana spotted like fish when I run. It's practical because it soaks up snot and sweat. It's whimsical because it's covered in the spot pattern of my favorite fish, brown trout. I like the idea of burying my face in fin when the wind kicks up dust and the miles pull down tears. And there are tears out here for sure. Blood too.

Reporter: You honestly can't feel those blisters on your feet?

Runner: I can't feel my feet, but I could still set the hook if I tricked a trout. Brown, brook, bow, it doesn't matter. To feel the tug of any or all would make my screaming feet shut up and my tiring heart speed up. Oh, how I wish I had a fly rod in my hand. I'm never in last place when I fish, but I'm in last place on this race. It's an awful, unexpected place to be.

Reporter: How many miles did you run while training for this sixty-seven-mile race?

Runner: It's sixty-two miles.

Reporter: Nope. Sixty-seven.

Runner: It is?

Reporter: This race is officially a 108K, not a 100K.

Runner: Whatever. I ran 636 miles while training for this race. Wonder how many hours I've spent wading? Not enough.

I could stay in this creek and skip the forty-whatever miles that are left. Dump out of this last-place predicament and end the assault.

Reporter: Last place is still a place. It's better than no place, but seriously. Last?

Runner: All those people I passed dropped out? Or did they pass me when I detoured to pee two hours ago? Or was it two minutes ago? Who cares. The sun is still up. My soak time is probably up, too. Get moving. I started before sunrise. I'll finish after sunset.

Reporter: Shadows are growing. You'll be running in the dark soon.

Runner: No worries. The black void doesn't haunt me like it used to. Hey, look at that rotting mine shaft. Some old fool thought that ghostly gap whispered of minerals and money at one time. One crazy time.

Reporter: Who in their right mind hauled ore from clear up here?

Runner: Not me. Well, I could. I'm up here. Running, not mining. Stumbling, really.

Reporter: I'm quickly discovering there's nothing natural about what you're asking of your body and your brain.

Runner: Trail running is stupid.

Reporter: Agreed.

Runner: I've lost pounds, inches, sleep, and sanity. I've lost a tremendous amount of family time, too. Training for an extreme sport is a selfish endeavor. I know that now. So does my family, but my intensity must make an impression. My son asked me to help him train for his first trail race. So there's that.

Reporter: Yes, there is that.

Runner: What was that?

Reporter: A buck. You spooked it with your clumsiness. Last runner coming through. Keep up.

Runner: Last. How? I planned. I disciplined. I suffered. I triumphed. I trained for six months for hell's sakes. Hell. I'm in it and I'm dressed in desperation.

Reporter: Suck it up. You're out of your mind. You are in last place. You're over your head, coming up short and out of control.

Stop.

Pee.

Shoot flowering meadow photo with phone.

Reporter: As soon as this bathroom break is over, so is the pity party. There's a lesson here, an ugly one. The life lesson is this: mental will and physical skill are not always on the same page. That doesn't make you weak; that makes you real. And when they're not in sync, you struggle in unimaginable ways, regardless of preparation.

Runner: This is a surreal experience that's hard to translate into words, but when you're deep in an internal battle, the adventure is magnified. The river is colder, the ridges are steeper, the wind is stronger, but you stay with it because the flowers smell better, the trees are greener, and the view is amazing.

Reporter: Bullshit.

Runner: A magnified experience holds secret glory when you know you're seeing the wild like most people will never see it. You're seeing it when you're suffering, and it's still magnificent in a way that thrills you.

Reporter: More bullshit, but you held it together for a minute there.

Runner: This is a stupid life lesson. I despise it. Quit poking me with it! I'm carrying enough crap. I don't need a load of lessons piled on top. You carry it. And why am I talking out loud to myself? It's pissing me off.

Reporter: The flies are really pissing me off. So is the wind. It's bulky adversity shoving us back the way we came without you relenting.

Runner: If that's true, why am I in last place? Such bullshit.

Reporter: Apparently you still know how to cuss, but you forgot how to count.

Runner: What mile is this?

Reporter: Stop counting. Start running.

Runner: How long has it been since I ate? What's in my feedbag anyway?

Reporter: I challenge you not to look.

Runner: Another challenge? Exasperating. Like with all challenges I choose to chew on, this stupid idea is a bit too big of a bite. The you're-not-built-for-this-kind-of-work club sneering over my shoulder. I'm doing the work anyway. Lock me out. Kick me out. Avoid me. Scream at me . . . (people and animals). Poop on me . . . (just animals). I'm not quitting the story.

Reporter: What's the story?

Runner: I'm the story.

Reporter: Don't be so self-absorbed. This isn't compelling. This is crazy.

Runner: True. This isn't nearly as heartbreaking as that dad finding his son's body right before my first live shot. This isn't as agonizing as that grandma losing her hold on her drowning granddaughter during my flood coverage. And this isn't as calamitous as that family losing everything in a trailer fire on the 10 p.m. news . . . for the third time. All vivid expressions of pain bleeding with tormented emotion across the screen. All awful stories, but all stories worth telling.

Reporter: And this is your story?

Runner: That's it! Flip into work mode. See this lesson for what I'd like it to be, a story. Shoot this story with the juice left on my phone and see the finish line with the juice left in my body.

Reporter: Your self-induced anguish on air?

Runner: Dumb?

Reporter: Not dumb. Real. Besides, it'll make you focus.

Runner: Am I even on the trail anymore?

Reporter: They're pulling flags ahead of you. They're moving faster than you!

Runner: I don't have faster in me. I don't have flags anymore either. I've lost the trail.

Stop.

Scream.

Shoot flagless expanse photo with phone.

Reporter: What's worse than last? Lost. Lost in the wilderness with an hour of light left. You've covered thirty-five miles in thirteen hours and you're still not good enough, strong enough, fast enough. What you are is disqualified.

Runner: This is not my fault. They pulled my flags. I missed the cutoff time because I got lost. I got lost because they screwed up. They lost track of me, the racer in last place who is now in a lost place because they took my trail markers. Damn them! This isn't my failure.

Reporter: You're blaming others now? Get it together. Come on, flags or no flags, you weren't finishing this inhumane amount of miles by deadline either way. Know your limits.

Runner: I've never missed a deadline, but I don't see the finish line, so I need to call this what it really is: failure. But in this case, failure is soul saving. It's the one pretty part in all of this ugly. It's the calm in this chaos. It's me doing the thing I want to do because I have the mental strength to try, even though the risks are nearly insurmountable. The reality is that mentally, I'm built for a 100K, but physically, I'm built for a 50K. Humble pie swallowed, ego obliterated, but the wild is relentless, so why shouldn't I be? Sure, I fear failing, but I fear quitting more. As much as I don't want to fail, I don't want to back down from a challenge even more. Quitting might save the body, but it won't save the soul.

PART III

Finding

BETWEEN BOYS

WHEN I'M NOT running herd on my legs, I'm running herd on my littles. I love my littles because they're turning out to be what I longed to be when I was little: wild, brave, eyes up. My kids don't know it, but they're helping me with my own transformation as I encourage them to grow into theirs.

My kids. That still sounds weird. I have kids! And I like hanging out with my kids. They're the kids my mother was sure I would never have. She even admitted to thinking my tubes were tied when I called her with news of my pending motherhood the morning after the puking-in-the-sagebrush incident.

Most of the girls I grew up with in Utah married right out of high school and started families, just as that "most likely" award predicted. The scenario is pretty common in the anti-premarital-sex/pro-sex-for-procreation-once-married Mormon religion. I waited until I was in my thirties to have babies, a whole decade beyond legal drinking age, so classmates I knew as a teen had their own teens by the time I had my first son.

Being that I'm the not-the-only child and the not-the-son child, my husband and I opted for two offspring without knowing the sex of either until they took their first breaths. There's no "only one" in our house and there's no "only son." We have two boys and I have a hand for each of them. I find myself between my boys often and I don't resent it.

I'm choosing this middle. I don't just fall here by birthing order; I purposely put myself here. Sometimes because they're wrestling while Dad's driving, I crawl in the back seat to wedge myself as the neutral space between.

Other times, the middle is more pleasant, especially when we snuggle watching movies, when we share pages of a book, and when we eat in, camp out, and fly-fish. Fishing middle is my favorite middle as a mom, wade or float. My boys have a healthy respect for their mother and Mother Nature. I know it when I fish between them. One picks flies; the other finds fish for those flies. My place is the connection of fly with fish, the cast. That's what I help them with once they see trout rise and choose bug patterns to tie on their lines.

I know this skill, casting. A mom who can cast, and cast well for that matter. Guides know a good arm and I hear I have one. I don't argue with this. Fly-fishing is a skill I learned at about the same time I figured out I could excel despite my tendencies to hide and do otherwise.

Fly-fishing puts no childhood baggage on my back. I'm not following anyone. Females, and their besties, are the minority in this sport. I'm not forcing the activity just to fit, either. There's no head caster like there's a head cheerleader in high school.

I forget all about fit when I run fly line through my fingers while river rolls around my knees. Well, I forget until I see surprised faces at the ramp. Everyone likes to watch a guy back a boat down a launching ramp with a trailer hitched to a truck. It's a tricky maneuver. And everyone is surprised when I step out of the truck and they realize the guy is a gal. Yes, I can back up my own boat. I row it, too. If ever a gold-medal moment, handling my drift boat would be mine.

Come to think of it, I could make my own gold medal. The foil cap on the bold, blazing red cow container in the milk bin on my porch is gold. Six jugs delivered every two weeks. That's a dozen gold medals a month. Those are mine, all of them.

Except for the ones I'll share with my boys. A gold foil cap for each son every time I don't have to crawl in the back seat to break up a road trip wrestling match. I'll give them golds when they're big enough to row my drift boat, too, hypothetically of course. They'll call me crazy lady more than they already do if I start handing out gold foil milk caps as medals.

They have no idea what that milk bin on my porch means to me, and frankly, I find beauty in their ignorance. I've done enough things right so they don't feel wrong. They don't know how sour the lame light-blue cow on a carton tastes. They don't know the shame of being different and having *different* be synonymous with *defeat*. They don't see shy when they see me on TV and they don't think about birds disappearing when they watch bald eagles talon the same fish we're throwing flies at.

BEAUTY IS A BEAST

STARING AT THE strong talons of "Power House" doesn't help me heal, so I turn on my left side, belly, right side. Nope, no relief in any direction. My leg is twitchy with new bone growth. To the back again it is.

I curve my spine in the C shape of half sitting/half lying. I spend so many hours, so many days, in this position that my butt bones ache and my shoulder bones are sore. In this position, I'm staring at walls again. To the left of my bald eagle portrait is "Beauty's Beast." It's an image of a buffalo calf standing close to its mom's belly. I shot the photo in Yellowstone National Park.

Yellowstone road trips are one of our family rituals. It's less than two hours north. The boys in the back seat lose their patience with each other no less than 274 times, but certainly less than the quarreling records set when we go three hours south to Salt Lake City.

With the park's West Entrance so close, we have the luxury of enjoying the nation's first national park before the tourists arrive. My husband and I bike Yellowstone with our boys before cars are allowed to enter in the spring. We camp there before Memorial Day, too. Then we avoid the park like the plague until October when the tourists leave and we have the park to ourselves again.

We know the best routes for big game. That's why we have ten-bear days. (Ten grizzly and black bear sightings in one day.) We know the best ice cream is in Mammoth, the worst bathrooms are at Paintpots, and wolfies always hang out in Lamar Valley. Wolfies are the diehards who watch wolves year-round.

We joke in good fun with the rangers about when they feed the wolves and how many years until deer become elk. Neither scenario really happens. We know this, but what does happen in the park isn't always good fun.

I have footage of a grizzly sow and two cubs eating an elk calf while an elk cow watches from a few feet away. The audio track has to be buried at zero when I edit the footage because all you hear is a ranger yelling, "Lady in the purple pants, move back," over and over again.

The scenario plays on repeat every summer when more than four million tourists visit Yellowstone. For many of those millions, it's a once-in-a-lifetime trip to one of the last undeveloped, and protected, places on the planet. Imagine the importance of that, being lucky enough to experience such a world. They plan well and pay plenty to get to the park, but usually their plan and pay doesn't include an education in wilderness etiquette.

While everyone has the right to access natural resources on public land in America, no one has the right to neglect those resources. Sadly, that happens in Yellowstone more often than you realize. Many park visitors get carried away with fantasy, and their trip turns fatal. Fatal for people and for animals.

In the case of Purple Pants Lady too close to the grizzlies, she's oblivious to the ranger's warning and keeps moving in for a front-row seat like she's at the movies, but this isn't the movies. Purple Pants Lady is making everyone and everything uneasy with her self-inspired invasion. A grizzly, especially a female with cubs, will kill you if you invade her family unit. She doesn't see you as another mom. She sees you as a threat. She's wild. And we must let her be regardless of how moved we are by what we see. Do not feed, touch, or take the wild. It is not ours to feed, touch, or take.

In another overbearing reach of human hands in a world only animals fully understand, a father-son pair pulled into Yellowstone's Lamar Buffalo Ranch with a bison calf in their back seat in May 2016. These two tourists thought the calf was too cold. Yellowstone is cold. We take winter coats regardless of the time of year and consider ourselves lucky survivors if we go one whole trip without wearing them. That calf was only going to see more cold as the short summer waned. Now it won't see any cold because returning it to the herd didn't work. The mom lost interest. The calf died.

Decent moms don't understand this. I'm a mother and I don't understand this. I'm also not a buffalo; I'm a human. Attributing human emotions to an animal doesn't work. I admit, I struggle with resisting the urge to do it, but I do it and so do my boys.

We have our own baby buffalo moment. No post-worthy proof provided, but the sight never leaves my mind. I know my boys remember it, too, because they mention it every time we stand on the banks of Yellowstone's Firehole River.

May 2011. It's a sink-'em-deep snow year. The drifts are so significant, we can't see the fire ring in our campsite let alone make a fire. It's cold as usual in the park, but it's not crowded and we count on that. Bourbon-colored bison calves are stumbling along with their herd across the river from us. We watch them while we skip rocks. My human nature picks up on the herd's maternal instincts. They keep their kids back behind them in the safe zone, just like I do. The babies nap while the moms stand guard. When the babies are hungry, the moms feed them. All seems right. Then the herd starts swimming and all goes wrong.

I sense trouble as soon as the first calf starts swimming. The current is too cold, too swift. The calf is flailing. The urge to rescue rages in me, but I stay put and so do my boys. The calf comes up for air then goes under again. This happens five times. My grip on my sons tightens. Jumping in that river in early spring is suicide. Why don't these hairy moms know that? What could possibly motivate an icy river swim that risks the lives of babes right now? Panic pitches high in my gut. I look to the herd. I don't know what I expect to see. A stop. A head turn. Something. I can't even pick out the mother.

On the sixth rise, I know it's over. The calf's shiny black nose isn't inhaling deeply anymore. It silently sinks. It doesn't surface again. I stand on the bank, crying. It's a horrible moment.

I realize I'm a hypocrite for expecting a human response from an animal just because I saw it guard its young like I do.

I look down at my boys and realize something else. Sometime during those gasping-for-life moments, my boys, with me in the middle, started holding my hands instead of me holding theirs.

"It's okay, Mom," my younger son says. "There will be more babies." While the older offers, "Think about something else. Anything else."

Easier said than done, but it will be done, eventually. I still see that calf's head going under every time I look at the Firehole River, but I don't cry anymore. A dynamic wiser than me was in play that day, I just know it. It doesn't make it easier, but it makes it right. Bison live in the place I visit. They know better.

Yellowstone is my backyard, but it is *their* home. We should respect their home and their right to survive in it as they see fit. It's unfair for us to try to control, or even fully grasp, what's going on among the animals. We've lost that right. We are not wild enough anymore.

MOM IN THE MIDDLE

IT'S THE FIRST night of class and the room is packed. Students sit at tables. Parents stand on the fringes. My two boys, not having a long enough drive for back seat wrestling before arrival, elbow each other on their way to an open table. I follow them while parental eyes follow me. I know adults are only here as chauffeurs for kids who can't drive yet, but I'm here for more. I pass up the parents and approach the table with my sons.

"Move over," my older son says to his little brother. "Let Mom have the middle."

Yes, middle. Put Mom in the middle. Middle is a good place for Mom. I'm of small stature, so maybe I'll blend in with the small bodies around me. That's what I'm hoping for, because this is the awkward moment I've thought about since I signed up for hunter education. It's the moment parents on the fringe realize I'm more than a driver, I'm a student. Sitting at a table means I'm admitting I don't know it all, and that's just not what adults do, but I passed up the online course for classroom time on purpose. I choose to put my ignorance on display so I can be among the target audience, the next generation of hunters.

My boys are barely old enough to take hunter education in Idaho, but I'm so over the age limit, I'm grandfathered in. Hunter education became a pre-hunt requirement after I was born, so I don't have to take it. I take it anyway. Perspective is good, and I want this perspective, even if no other adult wants to be seen sitting at the kiddie table.

Now, don't get me wrong: I know how to hunt, mostly. My job as an outdoor journalist requires me to spend a lot of time stalking the wild with sportsmen, but I'm usually the one with the powerful footage rather than the firing power. Even if I did hit my target true, I wouldn't know how to field dress it. That's why I'm here: knowledge. The more my kids and I know about our natural resources, the better off we all will be.

Idaho's hunter education program is divided into four sessions. Each includes lecture time and hands-on training. The first time we lie on our bellies with guns that won't fire, I spout some sarcastic line from *A Christmas Story* about Black Bart. No one older than ten laughs.

During the second session, we are studying a picture of a bulging bull elk tied across the top of a tiny hatchback. Our instructor asks us if that's legal.

Yes.

But is it ethical?

A small hand shoots into the air in the front row. It's Macy Thorp, age nine. She's applying for a spring bear hunt with her dad as soon as she graduates this program and turns ten.

"No," Macy says. "Because if someone drives by and they have a much, much, much smaller elk, it would hurt their feelings."

True. Bragging is bad form. So is displaying your trophy like a hood ornament and thinking your hatchback is actually going to make it out of the woods with all that extra weight.

Next question: What is the number-one threat to wildlife?

Being that my boys and I live in Idaho, the wildest of the West, the quick and loud answer coming from the back of the room is no surprise. "Wolves."

The smug student in me smiles when the instructor says, "Nope. Wrong answer." He asks the question a second time and the right answer comes from a voice on my left. Out of my own son's mouth: "People." He's correct, and I'm proud. People. Specifically, people and our urban sprawl developments. When the wild runs out of room, we will run out of wild.

We're a few hours into the third night of class and my youngest is fidgety. It's past his bedtime. We're all tired. He lays his head in my lap, but I can tell he's still listening. So are the other kids.

How do you identify a male pronghorn?

"Black cheek patches," we all say in unison.

Where do you always look before you decide to shoot?

Behind the animal.

The quiz continues.

A teenage boy two rows over often references trapping when he answers questions, and he's comfortable looking at kill shots. The preteen girl in the front row is not. Not yet, at least. She covers her face every time images of field dressing pop up on the screen. My son perks up for those photos. He has a new pocketknife he's itching to use, but first, safety.

Gun safety is a major part of the course, and this is the night we show our loading skills one by one to the instructor for approval. Some of the kids handle the firearms like they weigh more than them. All the naïve barrel waving going on makes me anxious. I'm used to being around people who know how to handle guns rather than people learning how to handle guns (myself included).

One kid, the one drinking enough soda pop to flood a fountain, can't hold still. He likes this part of the course, and it's obvious he's handled firearms. He flies through loading a long line of rifles and shotguns before I fumble through one. I know it's not a timed race, but I'm bugged by his younger proficiency and my older lack of it.

It's our last session. The final of four. Test time. My youngest sincerely asks me if he can sit close so he can see my answers. I'm mortified by his honest attempt at dishonesty, but I'm just as doubtful about my own answers. What if I guess wrong and fail us both? No way are we sharing. He's young for such serious studying, but he easily wins the game Memory every time we play. He's got this. No peeking. Besides, I have my own test anxiety to deal with. I haven't taken a test in decades and I've never taken a test with my boys on either side of me taking the same one.

An hour later we're done, and I'm watching our instructor mark tests with a red pen, the same kind of pen I use when I edit copy. My knees knock under the table. My older son taps a pencil on his chair. My younger son gives up and puts his head down. It's past his bedtime again.

The instructor starts handing out hunter-orange bandanas and beanies. You get both if you pass. My boys smile as bright as the blazing color in their hands and I'm right there with them when we realize we've passed. Not only do we have matching hats to wear in the woods, we also know the difference between black bears and grizzlies, how to load bolt and lever action rifles, and why you don't parade your harvest on your hatchback.

Later, the instructor shows me my test score: 100 percent. I don't gloat, but I'm pleased. That score means something to me. I earned that perfect score by putting 100 percent of my pride on the line and leveling the learning field between my boys and me. Along the way, I met some new hunters, most of them "much, much, much" younger than me. And I know

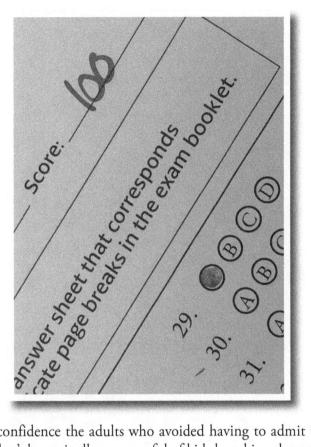

with confidence the adults who avoided having to admit that they don't know it all to a roomful of kids by taking the online course at home instead truly missed out on an experience worth dropping the grown-up façade for.

THE WADING GAME

"I BET THAT guy is staring at you because you're pretty," says my younger son.

Since I haven't brushed my hair, I bet that guy isn't staring because I'm pretty. He's staring because we're minorities. Woman with child. No beard among us. There's no way we know what we're doing.

But we do.

I reverse my truck into an informal parking spot, the only Idaho license plate on this dirt road. Locals lose Idaho's Henry's Fork of the Snake River to tourists in the summer. Can't blame the lot of them, really. The blue-ribbon fishery is known worldwide for prolific bug hatches and even bigger trout buffeting on those bugs. Plus, Henry's is in Yellowstone's backyard without the crowd, so you can imagine the appeal and the potential. I have valid reasons for living where some of the West's best water flows, and those reasons attract attention and visitors.

I turn off my truck and step out. I'm parked between Utah and Washington. Texas is two rigs over. My son hides his iPad under his seat just in case anyone in this fishy crowd has hot hands for electronics. Then he scrambles out of the truck, proclaiming he'll dress himself.

But he doesn't.

He doesn't even know which set of gear is his. He's passing a decade now, and his independence is innate, but he's fished his whole life either on my back or in my boat. This is his first time in waders. He's almost big enough to fit in one of the extra pairs I've been saving for him.

He says, "Why don't waders go to your neck?"

I tell him, "If water is up to your neck, you're not fishing, you're floating."

I unload two sets of waders and boots stashed among our mountain bikes in the bed of the truck. I brought two fly rods but I only string one. I'm no help to him if I hand him one rod while I walk off with the other. We'll share a rod so I have no reason to wander. He needs guidance with his cast, just as soon as I get him dressed.

I feel for my son's small feet inside large neoprene booties and shove them into wading boots before attaching gravel

guards. The garb keeps his feet and legs from freezing in the cold water. The getup is too big. His smile is bigger.

"Rock guards are legit," he says, hopping off my truck's tailgate turned dressing bench. "I need these for all my shoes. Especially my school shoes because I get rocks in them at recess."

Standing by the SUV next to us, Mr. Stare-Hard watches our circus with a scowl as the sun sets. He's the typical Henry's Fork angler, a bit heavy on weight and wrinkles. He's looking at us over magnified glasses sitting low on his nose. The kind of glasses too-aged eyes use to thread fly line through hook holes. The same eyes that have looked at me with unwelcome for as long as I've ignored the look and made myself welcome.

After decades of inviting myself to these outdoor galas, proving I can hang with the boys and that their story is so much better when I do, all I want to do is hang with my own boy. The boy who is oblivious to what I've worked on for years while warranting my place among men. I know my place, and it involves standing my ground. Staying is my stand, so I sigh at Mr. Stare-Hard but I don't budge.

When I don't act bothered by his scrutiny, he closes in and opens up. He's a white beard from Washington. His beard doesn't bother me, but his attitude does. He's been here a week. Based on his gripes, I can't figure out why he's still here.

"No flies. No fish," he says, still looking at us like we don't belong.

Oh, but we do. Of this I have no doubt.

I know there are flies. I also know there are fish. I caught my largest Idaho fish ever, a twenty-four-inch brown trout, on this water a few weeks ago. My BFF (big fish friend) Todd Lanning and I keep trading "remember when . . ." texts about it, so it's fresh on my mind for frequent flashbacks. There are fish in here for certain, but I keep that to myself and let my son cover the awkward pause of my silent reminisce.

"I wish there was a superhero who used a fishing rod," he says while turning away from Mr. Stare-Hard and aiming my rod case at some geese like it's a shotgun.

He continues to chatter like he has all day. He's a lot like me in that way, thoughts spilling out as fast as they sprout, subject-skipping with ease.

On our mountain bike ride earlier, we played genie. I wished for the banishment of all bad people. He wished for no Internet dead zones. We're both into video, me for my job as a journalist and him for his entertainment as a gamer. His devices, and mine, are now out of reach because we have fish to catch.

But we wait.

We watch from the bank. I hear sandhill cranes call in an ancient ruckus way off to my right while the river ripples over rocks like boiling water a few feet in front of my wading boots. At this spot, the river is less than a football field wide and no more than waist high all the way across. The gravel of its belly and the grasses on its hips are both significant signs of vitality. This is a healthy place. You can smell it. Abundant fish and flies with fertile land stirred in. It just smells right, a rare right. Many ecosystems don't smell healthy anymore, but this one does. I always breathe it in before stepping in a seam to cast.

Beyond where we stand gulping freshness, the surface of the water flattens. If a gulper rises, I'll see its head crack the calm. Mr. Stare-Hard, ready in breathable waders and fully stocked vest well ahead of us, is already standing in the river, but he's not watching ripples. He's watching us. I hear a gulp upstream. Mr. Stare-Hard can't hear it mid-river. I steer my son through knee-high grass and head upstream.

Mr. Stare-Hard smiles. It's possible he's amused by my son's jig along the single-track trail. He's taking hip-hop during hockey's off-season and he's grooving with excitement. But in all reality, Mr. Stare-Hard is probably smiling because he just realized we're not getting in the water next to him. I know better. He's of the no-dink-around crowd. We're here to dink around.

But we don't.

Five brown drake flies drift by. Three trout heads rise. Game on. We're in with one rod between us. I place my son directly in front of me. His head is sternum high. The scent of his hair seeps through his hat in a combination of bubbles, the bottle kind with a plastic wand, and gel. It takes a lot of styling product to Mohawk his hair when he's not wearing a hat.

I bury my nose in the top of his head. I've smelled hats since my first crush, BJ, in grade school loaned me his. I don't remember what it looked like, only what it smelled like. Bubbles. A hat worn by any boy long enough smells like bubbles. I've tested this theory so many times, I claim it as fact.

A few more years, maybe only one, and my son's head will pass mine, but for now I smell it then look over it. He's still short enough for me to watch what the fish are doing and keep him upright while he's fascinated over a new sensation.

"I feel like I'm in a bumble-beekeeper suit," he says. "Nothing can get in my shoes, and water compresses the sides of my legs. It feels awesome."

I'm a lefty. He's a righty. This is good. I wrap my left arm around his chest, tighten his back to my front, and guide his right-handed cast with my right arm. Right is my weaker cast. It won't take over like my left does. The softer touch works better for beginners.

A few casts in and he wants freedom. I'm thrilled he wants it and even more thrilled that he knows he can have it. I wanted it at his age, but I didn't know I could have it. I had enough fear for both of us growing up, so he has no need for it now.

I know the water is shallow enough for little legs, so I let him go. He steps a few feet from me and starts throwing line when the water meets his knees. His brightly dotted emoji ball cap throws color in the low light as he casts solo. I know, right in this moment, I will see this scene in my mental scrapbook forever. It's a keeper. The light, his laugh, my lack of concern for Mr. Stare-Hard downstream. All of it, mine by memory in the making.

His aim is true for short lengths. So is his attention span. He squats low to feel the current collect around his waist. His cast tanks with his dip, so he stands again, gathering himself for another swing. The line drops five feet in front of him. A fish rises to his fly. He's going to hook.

But he doesn't.

He casts again. I watch with all the wonder the moment is worthy of, gluing it to a page in my keep-this-one-close collection. He's got this. Fish or no fish, he's caught the magic and that's what matters.

It's last light. It's my son's first wade. Mr. Stare-Hard can stare all he wants. Maybe watching us will remind him why he really started wading way back when.

"When I grow up, I'm going to make my kid go wading with me instead of sitting around in the house playing video games," my son says when he heads to the truck in the dark with Mr. Stare-Hard long gone and griping about no fish at the bar upriver. "This is legit."

DIRT ROAD DANCE FLOOR

WE'RE HIKING THROUGH fall draped in winter, the first snow before the last leaf. We're scouting for elk ahead of hunting season. My husband and younger son are a few paces in front. Little brother, with his new casting arm, is chattering, singing, dragging sticks, and chucking rocks. He's doing everything his dad has an absolute hissy over when we're hunting instead of scouting. We shot targets before hiking, hoping it would level his hum, but he's still pinging high and hot after collecting spent shells.

Big brother is just the opposite. He's behind me with quiet presence. He's often in his own world and, man, I wish I knew what that world looked like, felt like. I'm sure it's fantastic. He's so aware of details, nuances, emotions. He tucks the best of what he studies inside his mind just like I did when I was little. He inherited my shy side. I see it in the way he stares at his shoes, like I did prepuberty when looking at laces seemed safer than looking at faces.

As I grew up, I grew out. I knew I had to if I was going to be a journalist. I knew that was my calling before I ever lifted my chin. I also had to get over my fear of beards. I run around with hairy faces in the forest when I'm on assignment. That was a no-go as a little girl. It's no problem now.

Kids are no problem either. I knew raising littles would be hard, but I didn't know it would be so much fun. They are a kick, especially in the sticks. It's one of the reasons why my husband and I added hook and bullet to hike and bike right about the time we added two boys to our household.

Raising kids in Idaho means our boys have access to huge swaths of public land. It's not rich man's land, it's everyone's land, and we can afford to play where there's no entrance fee, so our boys are backpackers, fly casters, gunslingers, and river rafters. Our family is well aware of the natural resources that accommodate our recreation and deserve our respect. At the end of one Middle Fork of the Salmon River trip, my older son said, "I haven't used a microwave for more than a week!" Mission accomplished.

Growing up, my family's outdoor pursuits were styled more for bonding with relatives than filling the freezer, so I only

hiked when I was little. And danced ballet. My dad was often late picking me up from practice. There I'd be in pink tights, satin-strapped pointe shoes twirling over my shoulder. The last ballerina balanced on the curb, waiting for a ride home, hair gathered into a clean, tight bun. I always hoped my dad would arrive before dark. Beards came out after dark. I didn't like beards or the dark back then.

Shaking off the knock of my ballet teacher's wooden stick pounding out a count of eight beats, I bring my head back to our scouting mission, listening to my son scuff his feet on the trail behind me. I know his head is down without looking back.

I often tell him, "Eyes up. Look at the world like you own it and you will." I don't remember my parents telling me that when I was young, but I felt it. If I could just figure out how to make eye contact, I'd make it. So will my son.

The gap between pairs grows as my husband and younger son take a familiar bend in the lower country. My husband, new to hunting, likes to hunt here. He was somehow lucky enough to draw one of fifty permits issued for this area two years in a row, but not lucky enough to put meat in our freezer yet.

He smells elk, hears them, sees them. They rub racks in deep canyons and push other elk over ridges. The wild herd is healthy and active in tough terrain fit for few people. My husband is one of the few, but he's convinced the elk know what's inside the range of an ethical bow or bullet shot, and they're always outside of it. It drives him delirious. I know that's what he's thinking about as he moves farther ahead, preoccupied, with little brother skipping to keep up as they look for Dad's elk and Son's rabbit.

Not one to obsess about being in the lead, my firstborn stops me and sticks out his fist. He's found a different hopper. A grasshopper, frozen in ice. Cue the quick thaw in my son's sweaty palm. Legs twitch as the bug heats to life.

It's a fascinating reveal, one I've never witnessed, and yet my son watches it with educated intentions like he's seen it happen before. Of course, he hasn't, but he instinctively understands the process. Apply cold, stop time. Add heat, revive life. He's never seen, or held, a frozen hopper, yet he knows holding it warms it. It's going to jump ship as soon as the cold evaporates.

My son rolls the bug in his hand, studying it, watching with his brilliant-blue eyes for what he knows comes next. His serious inspection is the same when field dressing upland birds and filleting cold-water trout. He transfers his worries into whatever he's working on. He's doing it now. Something is on his mind. It's going to be revealed soon. I stare at him as he stares at the hopper in his hand. I hold my breath as he expels.

"I can't dance."

"Sure you can," I say, making direct eye contact with him. "There's no such thing as *can't* in our house. There's *won't*, but not *can't*."

"Nope. In this case, I can't," he says, looking away from me and back the way we came. He's avoiding eye contact. "I watch you and Dad dance around the kitchen, but I don't know how to do that."

Now I look away. His confession is surreal. He doesn't know how to dance? We mean well as parents. We do what we think is best as parents, but my son just pointed out that my best isn't cutting it. Did I do that to my parents? If so, it feels awful. Just like me when I was a young daughter, my son wants something the parentals don't expect him to want. He wants dance lessons. In this arena, my younger son bravely declared his intentions like his dad always does. He wanted hip-hop. I found him a summer hip-hop dance class, but my older son isn't as vocal. I wasn't either before I figured myself out.

Damn, I missed my son's want just like my parents missed mine. Or maybe I never said what I wanted? Maybe hiding, rather than my parents with their different priorities, held me back. I honestly don't know what happened then, but I know what's happening now. In all my years of making sure my son travels every outdoor avenue, I forgot to transfer the extracurricular I endured as a kid. Dance. My son doesn't know how to dance.

His first junior high stomp is next week. Fast songs. Slow songs. Wallflowers. Party fouls. Just mentally revisiting those early teen years makes me anxious. Junior high is brutal but vital. That's when I crawled out of my own head and started looking up. My son is going to do the same thing, I just know it. But first, I need to help him with his want now that he's expressed it. That's more than I could do as a kid.

So, we dance. On a dirt road.

We've looped around and we're fairly close to our truck. I skip to it, open all the doors, crank the music, and move. Country, hip-hop, rock. My body is controlled when I mean it and crazy when I don't. My son watches, embarrassed, hiding a laugh behind a closed-lip smile. I know that smile. I have one, too, but I let it loose.

"Holler with a happy bellow," I tell him.

I grab his now hopperless hand and swing. He shows teeth.

The beauty of aging is the freedom that comes with giving up years. I care less about what others think and more about what I think. I run my life at an ambitious pace with an intensity for amplified adventure that wears most other people weary. I want him to know that kind of life and the emotions it brings before he's forty.

The last of the dry season clouds around our shoes, but neither of us is looking down. Eyes up, we're dancing. And laughing louder than the music. I know he won't dance like this at school, but he can out here. It's only the wild watching when you're shedding shy on a dirt road dance floor.

WORKING ON WHEN

THE SNOWY DIRT road we danced on is one of the newest images in my collection. It's in my office around the corner from the couch. My son and I are not physically in the photo, it's just the road, but I see us. I see me at forty-four and my son at thirteen, dancing with eyes up and laughs loud, the way I wanted to live when I was a little but learned to do much later in life.

Finding my place among men, especially among the three men I live with, is my proudest achievement in life. But I learned to find myself through nature first. That challenge, that discomfort of raw exposure within my own vulnerability, allowed me to stand strong and stay out there, way out there, where beasts and beards hide but I don't.

Of course, there are family portraits of us staged outside. I've taken those, too, but this one in my office, this empty road, is full of us. Two with born confidence ahead. The other two finding it through a dance in the dirt.

I think about that photo, that moment, for a few more minutes before looking out the window. Mother Nature has smothered Idaho in snow while I've been confined to the couch, growing bone.

While recovering, I've spent more time looking at my work than looking out the window, but as I look out now, the sun finds a hole in the gauzy clouds. It reveals itself at just the right angle, sending white light across the black couch. The clouds collect themselves to cover the sun's escaping rays. The movement causes a scan effect, like the bright light beam on a copy machine passing over a page for duplication. A sliver of sunny disposition passes from the top of my greasy, unkempt hair to the bottom of my leg on the mend. The leg I stand on when I document the outdoors.

I bet my husband had to shovel snow again today before he left. He had to return to work, his students with special needs needing him more than I do. I dressed myself, did my leg stretches, and then slid down the stairs, dragging my crutches with me to the couch.

I use them now to stand, bathroom break imminent. I lean on them as I start my trip through the house. Past the couch, the pictures, then through the kitchen. And what do you know,

from the kitchen I can already see the mudroom and beyond it, the half bath. Washer, dryer, baskets of beanies between.

My husband had to leave the house for the day, but he didn't leave me, and he didn't leave the swinging door closed. It's thoughtfully propped open just the way he knows I need it to be, so I can hobble through without hitting my head.

It's been two months since my right foot printed the earth's surface. It will be at least that many more months before the snow melts and my foot touches ground again, before I'll be out instead of staring at the outside from within. I'll be walking, eventually running, but in the thick of this challenge, I see no end. It's a good thing I know better than that. I expect more from myself than that.

I've learned life isn't about finding what's comfortable. It's about persevering through what's not. That's why I started Tight Line Media in 2006 as a freelance journalist. The stories in this book took place in the years since then. Most of my personal growth happened in the same chunk of years, the outdoors growing this girl like it grows all things meant to be wild and born to be free, even if they don't know it at first.

I had a fairy-tale ending planned for this book, me tent camping alone somewhere for final edits, the inspiration flowing uninterrupted from the river to these pages made of trees. As with all my well-intended, unreasonable expeditions, the end is nothing like that. I was foolish to think I could get away with scripting it. Just like Mother Nature, real life had other plans for me. It ripped me away from the distractions of parenting and producing, but it did so with violent upheaval and a smackdown on the couch. This long-term sit-in with a leg injury forced me to examine my place, to really see myself and my work from beginning to now.

My editors wanted professional failure and personal pain to give the book more significance, more substance. I adamantly blocked both as unnecessary smudges of awkward until my leg broke. Ten deeply soul-searching chapters gushed out when my medically induced drug days ended, taking two months of my short-term memory with it. I am not about to say learning to live with a rod in my leg is the best thing that ever happened to me—far from it—but the book is better for it. And so am I.

In my decades-long scramble to find my identity among mankind, I didn't realize I'd already found it in nature until I had to stop working hard enough, fast enough, and good enough.

This is the end of the book, but it's not the end of my story. There will be more misadventures in the wild when I get back out there. When. Not if.

AUTHOR'S ADVICE

"Work for it rather than wish for it."
—Kris Millgate

photo credit: Emily Stone

BIBLIOGRAPHY

Portions of these chapters appeared in stories for the following media outlets:

Part	Chapter	Outlet
II	Banding Baldies	KPVI: *Time OUT with Kris Millgate*
II	Illegal Eagles	Oregon Public Broadcasting
II	Seeking Refuge	National Wildlife Federation
II	Presence Lost	*Hatch* Magazine
II	Lone Woman in White	Idaho Public Television
II	Green with Envy	Trout Unlimited
II	Collaring the Wild	*East Idaho Outdoors*
II	Courting Bull Elk	Trout Unlimited

GRAND PATRONS

Adam Johnson

Andrew Del Greco

Bill Helm

Bill's Bike & Run

Brandon D. Hoffner

Brenda Stanley

Bryan Vohs

Catherine Hardy

Catherine Traverso

Chris Street

Christina Assante

David M. Smith

Dayne Dingman

Erin Claire Hanson

Gene Petty

Glenmore Haynes

Gray Augustus

Greg Ball

Gunnlaugur Guðleifsson

Hollie M. Miyasaki

Jackie Flowers

Jamie L. Loizzo

Janet Loxterman

Jennifer McElroy

Jimmy's All Seasons Angler

Joselin Matkins

Joshua Chamberlain Clark

JT Thompson

Kareen Freeman

Kathlene Millgate

Keegan L. Berrett

Keith Crowley

INKSHARES

INKSHARES is a reader-driven publisher and producer based in Oakland, California. Our books are selected not by a group of editors, but by readers worldwide.

While we've published books by established writers like *Big Fish* author Daniel Wallace and *Star Wars: Rogue One* scribe Gary Whitta, our aim remains surfacing and developing the new author voices of tomorrow.

Previously unknown Inkshares authors have received starred reviews and been featured in the *New York Times*. Their books are on the front tables of Barnes & Noble and hundreds of independents nationwide, and many have been licensed by publishers in other major markets. They are also being adapted by Oscar-winning screenwriters at the biggest studios and networks.

Interested in making your own story a reality? Visit Inkshares.com to start your own project or find other great books.

CPSIA information can be obtained
at www.ICGtesting.com
Printed in the USA
BVHW031211140719
553406BV00001B/56/P